On the Modernist Long Poem

Margaret Dickie

On the Modernist Long Poem

University of Iowa Press  Iowa City

University of Iowa Press, Iowa City 52242
Copyright © 1986 by the University of Iowa
All rights reserved
Printed in the United States of America
First edition, 1986

Jacket and book design by Sandra Strother Hudson
Typesetting by G & S Typesetters, Inc.
Printing and binding by Edwards Brothers, Inc.

Library of Congress Cataloging-in-Publication Data

Dickie, Margaret, 1935–
   On the modernist long poem.

   Includes index.
   1. American poetry—20th century—History and
criticism.   2. Modernism (Literature).   3. Epic poetry,
American—History and criticism.   4. Eliot, T. S.
(Thomas Stearns), 1888–1965. Waste land.   5. Crane,
Hart, 1899–1932. Bridge.   6. Williams, William Carlos,
1883–1963. Paterson.   7. Pound, Ezra, 1885–1972.
Cantos.   I. Title.
PS310.M57D53   1986   811'.52'09   85-20958
ISBN 0-87745-140-0

"And as to who will copy this palimpsest?"

Contents

Acknowledgments   ix

Abbreviations   xi

1. Introduction   1

2. *The Waste Land*   18

3. *The Bridge*   47

4. *Paterson*   77

5. *The Cantos*   106

6. Conclusion   148

Notes   163

Index   171

Acknowledgments

LIKE THE POEMS it studies, this book has had its own narrative of composition that has, among other things, generated debts and gratitudes. I started it during a semester's appointment to the Center for Advanced Studies at the University of Illinois, and later it was supported by funds from the University's Research Board. I am grateful for this aid. My colleagues Nina Baym and James Hurt both read and commented fully on an early version of this manuscript, and Laurence Lieberman, a writer of long poems himself, always provided cheerful encouragement. I was assisted by two extremely able graduate students, Nancy Barry at the beginning of the project, and Karen Ford at the end. And finally, much too late, I acknowledge the example of Hyatt Waggoner, who early taught me what I could then learn.

Versions of Chapter 2, "*The Bridge*," and Chapter 5, "*The Cantos*," appeared in *American Literature* (March 1985) and *ELH* (Winter 1984).

Abbreviations

THE FOLLOWING TEXTS have been used in this study and will be cited in parentheses by the abbreviations listed here.

Hart Crane, *The Complete Poems and Selected Letters and Prose of Hart Crane*, ed. with an introduction by Brom Weber (Garden City: Doubleday, 1966), HC; *The Letters of Hart Crane: 1916–1932*, ed. Brom Weber (New York: Hermitage House, 1952), LHC.

T. S. Eliot, *The Waste Land: A Facsimile and Transcript*, ed. Valerie Eliot (London: Faber & Faber, 1971), WL; *The Complete Poems and Plays: 1909–1950* (New York: Harcourt Brace & Co., 1952), CP; *Selected Prose of T. S. Eliot*, ed. Frank Kermode (New York: Harcourt, Brace, Jovanovich, 1975), SP.

Ezra Pound, *The Cantos* (London: Faber & Faber, 1975), C; *Selected Letters, 1907–1941*, ed. D. D. Paige (New York: New Directions, 1971), LEP; unpublished letters in Paige Collection of

Beinecke Library, Yale University; *Literary Essays of Ezra Pound*, ed. with an introduction by T. S. Eliot (New York: New Directions, 1968), LE; *Guide to Kulchur* (New York: New Directions, 1952), GK; *Impact: Essays on Ignorance and the Decline of American Civilization*, ed. with an introduction by Noel Stock (Chicago: Henry Regnery Co., 1960), I; *Instigations of Ezra Pound* (Freeport, N.Y.: Books for Libraries Press, 1967), In; *Selected Cantos of Ezra Pound* (New York: New Directions, 1970), SC.

William Carlos Williams, *Paterson* (New York: New Directions, 1963), P; *The Selected Letters of William Carlos Williams*, ed. John C. Thirlwall (New York: McDowell, Obolensky, 1957), SL; *Selected Essays of William Carlos Williams* (New York: New Directions, 1969), SE; *Spring & All* (Frontier Press, 1970), S&A; *The Great American Novel* (Paris: Contact, 1933), GAN; *The Autobiography of William Carlos Williams* (New York: Random House, 1951), A; *I Wanted to Write a Poem: The Autobiography of the Works of a Poet*, ed. Edith Heal (New York: New Directions, 1958), IWTWAP.

On the Modernist Long Poem

1 Introduction

EVERYTHING ARGUED AGAINST the writing of the long poem in the Modernist period, even the poems that were written. Yet the American Modernists all wrote long poems and struggled at length. T. S. Eliot started and set the style with *The Waste Land*. Hart Crane devoted his brief and Ezra Pound his lengthy creative life to the composition of a single long poem. And William Carlos Williams claimed to have had the idea of *Paterson* from the very beginning of his career, although he put off composing the poem until relatively late and then took some twelve years in the production.

It is not strange that such poets should be attracted to the long poem, since they were serious and ambitious, and the long poem is an attempt at the major poem. But it is curious that this particular generation of poets should be so attracted, because they had been committed in the beginning to brevity, intensity, imagistic precision, rhythmical rigor. A paradigmatic case is Pound, whose long poem sprawls over half a century of composition even when he argued that by great art he meant "something like 'maximum efficiency of expression'" (LE 56).

Actually, the composition of the long poem marked a second stage of creative activity for the American Modernists.[1] Their first efforts had been to reduce poetic form, purify language, and focus imaginative attention. The Imagist program of 1913 had encouraged the direct treatment of the thing, limiting the poet's role to the minimum requirements of a recorder. Although these poets soon moved beyond the restrictions of Imagism (and some, like Crane and Eliot, never subscribed to its more radical experiments), they remained attached to the Imagist tenets that encouraged a tightening of form. For example, Williams said that he hoped to "escape from crude symbolism, the annihilation of strained associations, complicated ritualistic forms designed to separate the work from 'reality'—such as rhyme, meter as meter and not as the essential of the work, one of its words" (S&A 23). Eliot, too, emphasized the importance to him of the intensity of art: "For it is neither emotion, nor recollection, nor without distortion of meaning, tranquillity. It is a concentration, and a new thing resulting from the concentration of a very great number of experiences which to the practical and active person would not seem to be experiences at all" (SP 43).

Escape from all that would strain form and extend it combined with concentration on the particular and minimum to make the long poem appear initially undesirable and unnecessary. Interest in the new would itself force attention to the short poem, with its potential for controlled experimentation. And because the Modernists identified the first task of modernizing as ridding poetry of its accumulated crudities, they needed to concentrate on the briefest form of expression, or rather they had greatest hope for success if they restricted their form, using not one word that did not contribute to the presentation.

This first stage of experimentation proved easier to achieve and establish than the poets had any reason to imagine. The Imagist program, Williams' playful Dadaist experiments in *Spring & All*, Crane's derangement of syntax and logic, Eliot's adaptation of Laforguean irony—all these quite different efforts at concentration—revolutionized immediately the opportunities for American poetry. This first stage of Modernism succeeded rapidly in American poetry not simply because these poets were resourceful and inventive and had no resistance from an older generation of accomplished poets, but because American poetry has had a tradition of experimentation and has been especially receptive to new movements. Whitman, Poe, and Dickinson, the major poets of the nineteenth century, had all been innovators.

But the rapidity with which Modernism revolutionized American poetry left these poets to live out the greater parts of their careers in a revolution that had succeeded. Self-conscious experimenters, they had either to try new experiments or to repeat themselves. They moved then, flushed with a sense of their own accomplishment, into a second stage of experimentation, an effort to take their trials with the brief, difficult, non-mimetic lyric, to the extreme by writing the long poem. This experiment changed the poets and redirected the Modernist movement from its beginning in radical experimentation in the short lyric to its end in the long public poem.

The history of Modernism from the Imagist platform of 1913 to the publication of *Drafts and Fragments of Cantos CX–CXVII* in 1969 remains to be written, but its bare outlines may be detected in the compositions of the long poems that span almost this full period. These poems, read separately in the order in which their parts were composed and together in the sequence in which they were published, reveal the development of Modernism from an iconoclastic and rebellious start in tense, complicated, and confused experimentation through a middle stage of exhaustion, accommodation, and revision, to a final acceptance of what the long poem had conserved and simultaneously, if paradoxically, to a longing for a conventional finish or coherence that had never been attempted. Modernism was not simply a descent from experimentation to convention, as the poets progressed from youth to age, but rather a movement of constant revisions in which the poets whose initial ambition had been to extend the resources of language found its limits and deepened the awareness of their own limits. As it revealed its energies in these long poems, Modernism became in the end a conservative or conserving movement, quite different from its revolutionary beginnings.

This understanding of Modernism has been obscured by isolated close readings of the long poems as independent, revolutionary experiments, each poem annotated and explicated as a unique accomplishment. Concentrating on the finished published poem, such readings have tended to confirm the sense of Modernism as a movement without an internal history. But the poems themselves have a history, a long period of gestation and development, in which they were revised and reconsidered and changed in structure and focus. Also, the poems together span a long history of composition in which Modernism changed and developed. It is this process which the long poem determined.

The long composition of the long poem reveals an inside narrative of each work. The narrative of composition, the continuous stages through which these discontinuous poems passed from idea to expression, may appear to reveal only the underside of the work, which, like the unfinished seam of a hastily sewed garment, was never intended for display. Such a narrative must, of necessity, lay bare the poet's uncertainty of purpose, his too certain ambition, his pretensions and doubts, his play and his trivializing, all finished over in the final form. And if that were all, it would not be enough. But these narratives of composition also reveal the tenacity of intention, the poet's enigmatic persistence against all odds toward the impossible poem, the unrelenting struggle with despair and failure to create and succeed. Unlike inside seams unfinished in sewing, the inside work of the poet is often on display in this finished work, often ragged and unsightly, but exposed by the poet, who seems blind to its lack of finish. The poet seems to retain his affection for the first insight long after he has had the second and third. Thus, the narrative of the poem's composition offers not only an important context in which to read the published poem, but, especially for the nonnarrative long poems of the Modernist movement, it may provide the necessary narrative component of the poem itself.

More than that, the narratives of these quite different poets and their poems' compositions have peculiar affinities that bear examination. It may be considered preposterous (and certainly has been by early readers of this text) to suggest that the composition of a relatively short long poem like *The Waste Land* has anything in common with the extended composition of *The Cantos*, that *Paterson* and *The Waste Land*, so intentionally at odds with each other and composed under such different circumstances, could be related. The resistance to the idea that these compositions are related may be in part just good common sense, but it has been stiffened by a view of American Modernism as a collection of isolated and disparate poets working independently and often at cross-purposes. That they were, but insofar as they shared the ambition to write the long poem, they shared too the dilemma of form that it presented for their generation and, even more, the inadequacy of private and purified language to shape the public themes which they aspired to address.

To trace the stages through which each poet worked toward the finished or at least finally published long poem will offer, if not a single narrative, at least a series of similar difficulties that the poets both created and assumed as Modernists. In the poetic solutions to those problems as they were developed by each poet over time, the Modernist long poem and its sense of form evolved. The term itself, *the long poem*, will need some justification at the start.

The long poem, for all its inadequacies as a designation, has the merit of distinguishing the salient feature of this otherwise unidentifiable genre. Epic and various permutations of that term—*proto-epic* or *pre-epic*—have been appropriated both by the poets and their critics as useful classifications. They too point to the length of the Modernist long poems, but they point to other qualities as well, all absent from the Modernist long poem, that require extraneous explanation. In the same way, *the poetic sequence*, another term for the long poem, obfuscates more than it clarifies, since *sequence* suggests an order of development nowhere evident in these poems' compositions. Bare and simple as it is, *the long poem* as a term identifies nonetheless the single feature that most attracted the poet and made his work most problematic. Long in the time of composition, in the initial intention, and in the final form, the Modernist long poem is concerned first and last with its own length. This fact, as true of *The Waste Land* as of *The Cantos*, determined the poems more centrally than *From Ritual to Romance* or Douglas's economic policies. The term thus focuses the interest of this study not only on the long form but on the long process of composition through which these poets moved to find the form.

The shift from the lyric to the long poem was not made swiftly or easily, and in individual careers it often started poorly. For example, Eliot began to write a city poem in the tradition of urban satire and found it unwritable. It offered him nonetheless a start in the direction of the public poem. If *The Waste Land* became more complex as he undertook its composition and revision, it still had as its subject the culture it surveyed and judged. The turn from the private ruminations of Prufrock to the public world of urban satire was negotiated with a certain awkwardness and uncertainty in Eliot's career, but it pointed the way for the poetry that would come. After *The Waste Land*, and probably because of Eliot's success, his contemporaries began to announce their intentions to write long, public poems.

Pound had even greater difficulty than Eliot in getting started on his long poem. He had been writing cantos before the publication of *The Waste Land*, acknowledging that "one should not do the same thing all the time. The long poem is at least a change" (SL 115). Announcing that he was working on a poem of 100 or 120 cantos, he told his old teacher, Felix Schelling, "I am perhaps didactic; so in a sense, or in different senses are Homer, Dante, Villon, and Omar, and Fitzgerald's trans. of Omar is the only good poem of Vict. era that has got beyond a fame de cénacle. It's all rubbish to pretend that art isn't didactic. A revelation is always didactic. Only the aesthetes since 1880 have pretended the contrary, and they aren't a very sturdy lot" (SL 180).

Pound had difficulty in establishing his own sturdiness largely because, at this point in his career, he teetered between didacticism and aestheticism. Hart Crane, too, had trouble fulfilling his announced intentions. He sometimes lost faith in his convictions, but he too saw himself as a poet of public stature, trying to articulate a faith for a world he judged as "so in transition from a decayed culture toward a reorganization of human evaluations" (HC 218). He said: "I feel persuaded that here are destined to be discovered certain as yet undefined spiritual quantities, perhaps a new hierarchy of faith not to be developed so completely elsewhere. And in this process I like to feel myself as a potential factor" (HC 219). In writing *The Bridge*, he claimed that "thousands of strands have had to be searched for, sorted and interwoven" (LHC 305).

Williams was no less far-ranging in his ambition for *Paterson*, claiming that "the longer I lived in my place, among the details of my life, I realized that these isolated observations and experiences needed pulling together to gain 'profundity'" (P vii). He continues:

> It called for a poetry such as I did not know, it was my duty to discover or make such a context on the "thought." To *make* a poem, fulfilling the requirements of the art, and yet new, in the sense that in the very lay of the syllables Paterson as Paterson would be discovered, perfect, perfect in the special sense of the poem, to have

it—if it rose to flutter into life awhile—it would be as itself, locally, and so like every other place in the world. For it is in that, that it be particular to its own idiom, that it lives. (P viii)

This start in an intention to write a long poem distinguishes these poems from various long poems that develop as open form or sequences such as Walt Whitman's *Leaves of Grass*. These Modernist long poems are not sequences in the sense that they were composed casually, one poem added to another in a random process of development. The idea of a single poem was present in the poet's mind, even in Pound's mind, from the start of the work. Nor are these long poems sequences in the sense that they were composed in the sequence in which they were published, one poem calling up the next in successive voyages of discovery. The sections of these poems were written as the poets responded to a variety of creative opportunities and a range of inspirational moments. Work on the poem could start with the final section or with some middle point, or several different sections could be composed simultaneously. Sometimes the sections were created to fit into a preliminary outline, and sometimes the composition of the sections forced the poet to reconsider the whole poem he imagined he was writing. But the sections as written and as published follow two quite different sequences. These haphazard methods of composition were permitted by the poets' initial sense that they were writing long poems.

In addition, the long poem was to be a new experiment not only with form but also with poetry as a public language. The poets declared that their long poems were to be celebrations of the city, models for good government, values and visions by which to live.[2] Openly didactic, the poets set out to teach not necessarily difficult lessons, but simple precepts that required new and complex forms of expression responsive to the conditions of the modern world. Awareness of the impossibility of such a task was delayed by the poets' initial enthusiasm and confidence in experimentation, by their ambition and innocence. Their strategies differed. Eliot and Pound began by adapt-

ing older models of public poems to modern usage. Crane
trusted to inspiration and Williams to the materials of his world
to stock the capacious long poem. That they all foundered almost immediately suggests the inadequacy of their beginnings.
Still, they did not simply abandon their long projects then, but
rather stopped, waited, and began again. This persistence against
their initial difficulties and the different ways in which they
undertook to recommence unsteadied their poems, as the narratives ahead will explain; but as a common tactic of all these
poets, it emphasizes both the poets' unrelenting intentions to
create the long poem and paradoxically their willingness to
learn from the composition the requirements of form.

At the beginning, these poets had a firm if untested conviction in their own experimental powers, and a peculiar confidence in the power of art or in the discipline of the long form to
sustain them. In a commentary on Henry James' work which
echoes his own hopes, Pound says,

> I take it as the supreme reward for an artist; the supreme return
> that his artistic conscience can make him after years spent in its
> service, that the momentum of his art, the sheer bulk of its pro-
> cesses, the (*si licet*) size of his fly-wheel, should heave him out of
> himself, out of his personal limitations, out of the tangles of hered-
> ity and of environment, out of the bias of early training, of early
> predilections, whether of Florence, A.D. 1300 or of Back Bay of
> 1872, and leave him simply the great true recorder. (LE 299–300)

The depersonalization of the long work and of art itself which
Pound praises here had its strange and contradictory appeal for
all the Modernists. For these experimental poets the attraction
of the long poem was precisely in the "bulk of its processes,"
which might ease the pressure for constant experimentation
and still permit the largest experiment. But length, even that
briefly achieved by adding one word or line to another, revealed
swiftly its tendency both to inhibit expression and to restrict
experimentation.

Nonetheless, the Modernists early abandoned the long poem

to its long composition, as if, in the creative process itself, the form and content would become clear. Pound claimed of the elements he had presented in his first eleven cantos, "I hope, heaven help me, to bring them into some sort of design and architecture later" (SL 180). Justifying the time he was taking to write *The Bridge*, Hart Crane wrote, "It has taken a great deal of energy—which has not been so difficult to summon as the necessary patience to wait, simply wait much of the time—until my instincts assured me that I had assembled my materials in proper order for a final welding into their natural form" (LHC 305). And, commenting on his experience in writing a part of *The Waste Land* that went along with unusual speed, Eliot mentions the suddenness with which a work meditated for months or years can take shape and form. The intended length of a poem might then initially inhibit expression, but paradoxically have a creative power of its own. It might constrict the experiment with which the poem started in order to engender a different experiment. But most significant here is the extent to which these experimental poets came to rely on the gifts of expression allowed by the length of the long poem. The language eased, the words took form, and if the long poem did not write itself, the poets at least appeared to trust in such unpremeditated writing.

The public poem of the Modernist movement came early to depend upon the private inspiration of the poet. The process of art remained a mystery to these poets, or rather they kept from the start a reverence for the mysterious movement of creativity, the imaginative associations that could emerge without deliberate intervention, what both Crane and Eliot called the "logic of metaphor." On another level, and in opposition to this reliance on fits of creation, the Modernists read books of cultural anthropology, ancient texts in Latin or Provençal, geological charts of cities, and obscure historical tracts, in preparation for the long poems they intended to write. For every poet here, the inspired writing and the studious reading made uneasy combinations, and the long poem that emerged from this activity ricocheted between the two.

Neither inspiration nor preparation could obscure the almost immediate realization that the form and the content of the poem had to be developed in a much more deliberate process of composition. The long public poem has traditionally thrived on narrative or on argumentation for development, and the Modernists had no enthusiasm for either mode of expression. They intended to start the long poem with an image, a symbol, a fragmented translation, a mood of ecstatic affirmation. In short, they began to write the long poem as if it were to be an extended lyric. In *Paterson's* opening, the city which Williams takes as his subject is reduced to an image, the giant asleep beside the park. Crane makes Brooklyn Bridge into a symbol of bridgeship. Pound does give his poem an epic opening, but only by translating a brief section from *The Odyssey* into alliterative verse, as if he would display his talents as a philologist while he waited for his own poem to begin. These openings were alike in lacking a principle of development. Complete in themselves, the first sections of the long poems the poets wrote could be easily extracted as separate, finished poems. They announced no subject for development, promised no revelations, and offered no opening into the work ahead.

The Modernist long poem started then with a beginning that could not begin and a sense of structuring that had immediately to be dismantled or overcome. It was a different process for each poet. Williams, gathering together his particulars, imagined that he could make a start there, although he soon came to realize that the particular does not reveal the universal, that only the poet can make such a revelation. And much later he discovered that, as a poet, he did not have a talent for such work. Pound, poring over his texts, imagined that he was collecting evidence, although he came eventually to understand his enterprise as analysis and dissection, and later still as judging and summarizing. Crane fell back from his sweeping vision of the bridge into a studied effort to conceive the links between beginning and end and a final cry of anguish at his pains. Like Williams and Pound, he too had to revise his sense of purpose and to acknowledge the time he had taken to write and time itself as a donor of meaning. Eliot started with one model, and finding it unworkable moved to another in order to compose the long poem that retains the precarious form of its troubled composition.

The Modernists' initial difficulties were only partly formal, although even these difficulties have gone unacknowledged in the critics' ready acceptance of the poems' revolutionary status. Joseph Frank's classic definition of Modernist form as "based on a space-logic that demands a complete reorientation in the reader's attitude toward language" does not take into account the composition of the Modernist long poem. Frank claims that "instead of the instinctive and immediate reference of words and word-groups to the objects or events they symbolize and the construction of meaning from the sequence of these references, modern poetry asks its readers to suspend the process of individual reference temporarily until the entire pattern of internal references can be apprehended as a unity."[3] But the Modernist long poem, as it was composed, never had an "entire pattern" that could be apprehended as a "unity" at any point in its creation. Disunity, an inability to gather and order materials, a constant revision of purpose—these are the frustrations that hounded the poets as they wrote. They may have hoped that a "space-logic" would take over the poem, but they themselves remained unaided by it.

Frank's idea of form comes from the Imagist beginnings of the movement and from Pound's definition of the image as "that which presents an intellectual and emotional complex in an instant of time." But it was precisely an awareness of the limits of this sense of form that drove Pound and his contemporaries to attempt the long poem and kept them at the project with relentless ambition for half a century. The "intellectual and emotional complex" that they aimed to express demanded more than an instant of time to grasp, to compose, to comprehend.

As Frank himself admits, the American Modernists did not follow Mallarmé in his radical dislocation of the temporality of language. Rather, in their aspiration toward the long poem, they embraced not only time but the time-logic of language. Clearly, the requisite continuity even of a discontinuous long poem takes place in time. The appeal of the long poem appears to be the point at which these Americans, influenced by European and English models, still held fast to a native idealism. The sense of the whole—the idea that the greatness of the poem lies in the greatness of its theme—was a heritage of idealism that the American Modernists never abandoned. Even Williams, enthusiastic as he was for particulars, still aimed to write about something larger than the birds and the flowers. He wanted not just an image, but an image that would embody the whole knowable world.

But greatness of theme evaded the Modernists even as they aspired to it. Eliot's mixed reactions to the modern city—his irony and his anguish—kept him always open to his poem's composition and interpretation. Even late in his life, when he tried to settle his relationship to the poem, he could keep both reactions in view, saying, "Various critics have done me the honour to interpret the poem in terms of criticism of the contemporary world, have considered it, indeed, as an important bit of social criticism. To me it was only the relief of a personal and wholly insignificant grouse against life; it is just a piece of rhythmical grumbling" (WL 1).

Pound, whose work on *The Cantos* was an intolerably protracted and irredeemably frustrated search for the great theme of historical interpretation, admitted at the end of his life that he had still to "clarify obscurities" and "make clearer definite ideas or dissociations" because "an epic is a poem containing history. The modern mind contains heteroclite elements. The past epos has succeeded when all or a great many of the answers were assumed, at least between author and audience, or a great mass of audience. The attempt in an experimental age is therefore rash."[4] Defeated by time and by his own experiments as its recorder, he moves toward the end of *The Cantos* with the regret that "what you depart from is not the way" even when he must ask, "what whiteness will you add to this whiteness / what candor?" (LXXIV 425).

The long poem, which seemed at the beginning of its composition an open and capacious form for a theme that remained to be developed, revealed not only its limits but the inability of form to generate content. In *Paterson III*, Williams has to acknowledge that his dream "seems beyond attainment" (P 140) and, at the end of his writing on *The Bridge*, Crane is "impassioned with some song we fail to keep" (HC 111). *Dream* and *song* are odd words to identify the poems Williams and Crane set out to write, and they refer not to the poet's failure to celebrate the local or to write the myth of America—that is, not to the poet's failure of subject—but rather to his failure of inspiration. The dream and the song belong to the art world of poetry, to the inner imaginative life of the poet, and not to the public life of Paterson or of American history that Williams and Crane announced as their subjects. Yet, even in these long poems the dream and the song long outlasted the public subjects toward which the poets turned for materials.

Paterson, the city as a subject, proved intractable, remaining resistant to the poet's celebratory imagination. Williams' dream "to find one phrase that will / lie married beside another for delight" is the dream of form, but it is also the dream of marriage between the poet and his world and of marriage in that world. *Paterson*, as Williams worked on it, disappointed that hope partly because Williams lacked the resources to imagine it and partly because the world offered no evidence to support such a hope. The violent, iconoclastic, destructive poet of *Spring & All* did not turn suddenly tolerant and generous in *Paterson*, despite his celebratory dream. Williams' imaginative energies remained judgmental and diagnostic at least throughout the composition of the first four books of *Paterson*. His dream of marriage was then a self-deluding dream that reflected a certain denial of what Williams himself knew of the particulars of his world.

Williams' difficulties with his subject are unique. They emerged from his frustrated effort to write a public poem from a private dream, to write over what he knew, to develop beyond rebellion and judgment to celebration, even when his instincts and talents were all in the other direction. But his contemporaries had equal difficulties in finding the subjects of their long poems. The middle stages in all these narratives of composition struggle with the inadequacies of the beginning that allowed the randomness of the long poem with no inevitable development.

Every long poem will defeat its creator. Even Virgil was prepared to destroy what he imagined to be his unfinished poem. But for the American Modernists the long poem provided unusual hazards to extended composition because it had no principle of generation, no limits to reach or transgress, no narrative to tell, no hero to tell it. More than that, as Pound notes, there was between the poet and his audience neither a common language nor assumed answers. The American Modernists had everything to create in creating the long poem.

Such freedom posed certain problems for poets committed to experimental poetry. The public language they needed for the public themes they would address was to be refined by experiments designed to separate the poet's language from the public's. With this uncommon language, the poets had still to discover in the conventional public subjects that they addressed—the city, the myth of America, the local, the "repeat in history"—the new subject that would justify the long poem. These poets, each responsive to Pound's dictum "Make it new," aimed to make new or renew an awareness not of an esoteric art world but of the familiar world. The contradiction between the revolutionary enthusiasm for the new and the attachment to a social, historical, and political reality produced poems in which complicated and difficult forms that appear to defy any mimetic function are nonetheless committed to a world that may be itself complex and unclear, but is neither unknown nor new.

In their poems, the Modernist poets addressed the world in which they lived. Frank's idea that the reference of any word-group in the Modernist poem is to something inside the poem is only partially correct. These poems are indeed self-reflexive, but self-reflexively concerned about their inadequacy to express, address, and refer to an objective world. Perhaps the most private and elusive of these poets, Crane was also the most anguished that his vision was not adequate to the facts of modern life. Pound's obscurities of expression can be interpreted as a willful retreat from communication and a disdain for the world he judged, but he imagined himself as a poet addressing a world that desperately needed his clarity of vision and his sureness of judgment. Far from cutting off the referentiality of words, he was engaged in a constant clarification of his references. If his long poem circles back to words, details, and obsessive moments, it is not so much because he puts his trust in "space-logic," but rather because he has in the logic of time come to a fuller understanding of what it was he wanted to say.[5]

It is true that, as the long poem progressed, it grew more self-reflexive, but curiously this self-reflexivity reflected not a complete reorientation in the attitude toward language nor a new conception of the subject of poetry. Rather, it served to express the poet's late conservative desire for a different poem from the one he had completed, a lesser effort, and, in his final exhaustion, a more easily satisfying work. The final judgment of the poet on his work, expressed in self-reflexive commentary, had little to do with the actual poem he had created. It pointed instead to an idea or design that had failed, even when such a design had been nowhere apparent in the narrative of composition or in the actual composition. For example, Pound calls at the end for "A little light, like a rushlight / to lead back to splendour" (*CXVI* 797). And Williams maintains, "The dream is in pursuit!" (P 222).

The splendor grew as the poems grew, and the idealization of form in this splendor forced the poets to devalue the poems they had actually written and to overvalue the dreams with which they thought they had started. At the end of these long compositions, Pound, looking backward, and Williams, looking forward, are gazing at the same unattained object—the whole poem or the poem as a whole that they now imagined they had set out to write. That they had never had such a poem in view is only part of the melancholy of their mood. The gift of the long poem and the "bulk of its processes" had been to make these poets realize their limitations as great true recorders even as they were leaving the great true recordings they had composed.

Pound launched out from *Canto I* with the confidence of the experimenter: "So that:" He ended more surely:

> Two mice and a moth my guides—
> To have heard the farfalla gasping
>   as toward a bridge over worlds.
>
>   .   .   .   .
>
> To be men not destroyers
>   ("Notes for CXVII *et seq.*" 802)

The movement between these lines details a narrative of composition that can be traced in Pound's career. Although Pound's work has the longest span, the works of Eliot, Crane, and Williams reveal their own narratives now to be detailed. To read each long poem as it was put together is to see each poem as a developing work and each poet as a tireless experimenter even as he moved in a conservative direction. Together, the compositions of these poems compose the history of Modernism, and from them may be derived the concluding narrative of the movement itself. "So that:"

2 The Waste Land

THE WASTE LAND was the first long poem of the Modernist experiment. The narrative of its composition, evident in its published drafts, underscores an uncertainty of purpose, a dilatory progress, and a divisive organization. Yet the poem had an immediate impact on Eliot's contemporary poets, forcing them to reconsider their own work and inspiring this generation of lyric poets to try the long form in order to test their strength and contest Eliot's dominance. The originality of *The Waste Land*, as well as its originary status, inheres in its openness, its receptivity to completion, its tentative structure—all properties of its length that plagued Eliot in the writing and inspired his fellow poets to finish the poem in their constructive readings, yet moved them to equal if not quite similar creative difficulties.

The history of the Modernist long poem was outlined very early in the initial reactions of Eliot's contemporaries to *The*

Waste Land. Ezra Pound, the poem's first and most enthusiastic reader, went back to work on *The Cantos* after reading and editing *The Waste Land*. As he recommenced his own long poem, Pound became more assertive about its possibilities, claiming, "Perhaps as the poem goes on I shall be able to make various things clearer. Having the crust to attempt a poem of 100 or 120 cantos long after all mankind has been commanded never again to attempt a poem of any length, I have to stagger as I can" (LEP 180). He had earlier admitted his envy of Eliot's achievement by confessing, "I am wracked by the seven jealousies and cogitating an excuse for always exuding my deformative secretions in my own stuff, and never getting an outline. I go into nacre and objets d'art" (LEP 169). Once Eliot's poem was published, Pound called it "the justification of the 'movement,' of our modern experiment, since 1900" (LEP 180), thus acknowledging its double value for him—it freed him from the immediate need to justify the Modernist experiment by his own long poem, and it set a standard which he could imitate and exceed. Pound had cautioned Eliot against adding to *The Waste Land*, which he called "the longest poem in the English langwidge" (LEP 169), but its completion encouraged him to project the much longer poem of one hundred cantos. If *The Waste Land* inspired Pound to return to work on *The Cantos*, it also allowed him the leisure of a lifetime to complete his long poem.

In contrast, Hart Crane took immediate issue with *The Waste Land*. Writing to Gorham Munson, he said: "What do you think of Eliot's *The Wasteland*? I was rather disappointed. It was good, of course, but so damned dead. Neither does it, in my opinion, add anything important to Eliot's achievement" (LHC 105). Crane determined to "take Eliot as a point of departure toward an almost complete reverse of direction" (LHC 114) and started at once to project his own long poem, *The Bridge*. The initiating symbol of his poem came out of Eliot's wasteland but could be used, Crane imagined, to represent wholeness and harmony, the opposite of Eliot's broken images. This impulse to affirmation was quickly and seriously tested in the writing of *The Bridge*, but it had sufficient impetus to launch the work that was to absorb Crane for the rest of his life.

William Carlos Williams shared Crane's enthusiasm for a celebratory poem, but he differed from Crane in his estimate of Eliot's achievement. Williams objected not so much to the pessimism of *The Waste Land* as to its erudition. That poem turned poetry back to the library just as it was making an exit to the world, Williams claimed. Although he could conclude of Eliot's work, "It forced me to be successful" (IWTWAP 30), actually it took almost twenty-five years for Williams to write *Paterson*, the long poem in which he was to make, he announced, *"a reply to Greek and Latin with the bare hands"* (P 2).

During this interim, Williams diverted his attention from poetry, trying other forms of expression—novels, history, short stories, plays—as if he were seeking in every genre but poetry the means of longer form. Finally, he turned to the long poem, claiming that he had had it in mind since the beginning of his career, although in a lifetime of immense productivity, this poem refused to form itself. Like Eliot, Williams had uncertainties of conception and purpose which troubled him the more because he imagined he had made accommodations for them in his open and generous conception of form. Pitting himself against Eliot, Williams found nonetheless that he could not escape the creative dilemmas he had mistakenly attributed to Eliot's erudition.

The Waste Land, the long poem that initiated this complex history of long poems, has its own unique history of composition, but it also shares with the poems that were to follow a creative struggle with long form. Obscured by the poem's immediate success and by the authority with which Eliot's first readers endowed it in order to seal off its accomplishments, this struggle reveals nonetheless the basic confrontation between a poet's experimental energies and the conventional requirements of any long form. Uncovered, the struggle of its composition places *The*

Waste Land not in opposition to the long poems that were to follow but rather first in this long line of experimentation. Shorter than *The Bridge, Paterson,* and *The Cantos,* and written in a much more concentrated span of time, still *The Waste Land* offers in brief an outline of the creative struggle that was to be repeated again and again as these widely divergent poets faced the dilemma of long form. The poem has brief and isolated narrative passages which readers have attempted to put together by imposing various schemes for a sustained narrative. In this effort, they suppress the narrative of composition embedded in the poem, to which we may now turn.

T. S. Eliot planned to write a long poem as early as November 1919, and his New Year's resolution for 1920 was, he wrote to his mother, "to write a long poem I have had on my mind for a long time" (WL xviii). By January 1922, he had submitted to Ezra Pound for comment the drafts of what Pound called "a damn good poem (19 pages)" (WL xxii). In June 1922, Eliot announced his intention to add footnotes to the poem, and by November he could claim, "As for *The Waste Land,* that is a thing of the past so far as I am concerned and I am now feeling toward a new form and style" (WL xxv).

This period of composition was brief and, to all appearances, purposive, but the long poem that emerged had undergone an intense, if contracted, crisis of conception in which its form was revised and its purpose altered. *The Waste Land* is layered with divergent intentions compressed together only by the single intention to length. It started out as one kind of poem, transformed itself into another, as Eliot and then Pound worked over its sections. One of its achievements is its existence as the long poem that it started out to become. In this, *The Waste Land* testifies both to the tenacity of form itself in the face of every experiment and change, and at the same time paradoxically to the persistence of experimentation in finding its adequate form.

In order to start a long poem, the poet must have some idea of how he will complete the work, and Hugh Kenner has argued convincingly that *The Waste Land* began as an urban satire.[1] The first sustained work on the poem was the seventy-two-line opening of "The Fire Sermon," written in the style of Dryden or Pope which Eliot eventually abandoned. If this form proved inappropriate for Eliot's purposes, it was sufficient to start the poem, and it led eventually to a more congenial form. In fact, it may have been the failure of this section to complete itself that inspired Eliot to another mode. Before Pound marked through the section, commenting "too loose," "rhyme drags it out to diffuseness" (WL 39), Eliot had broken off the proposed narrative of Fresca with the pointed question, "From such chaotic misch-masch potpourri / What are we to expect but poetry?" (WL 27).

This question marked an unexpected turn in Eliot's treatment of Fresca, who was transplanted immediately from the eighteenth-century model to the self-inflicted irony of Pound's "Hugh Selwyn Mauberley." The form proved no more useful than Pope or Dryden, nor more workable for Eliot than for Pound, who had also used it to deal with a subject about which he had not made up his mind. Finally, Eliot's impatience with his own dilatory movement breaks through the line that he will pick up in the next section, one that will eventually develop a motif of the finished poem: "But at my back from time to time I hear" (WL 27). With that line, Eliot advanced into the poem he was to write. The composition of the Fresca section had had its benefits: the exhaustion of an unusable style and subject, an unwilling awareness of that fact, and this line which freed Eliot from the deadlock of the heroic couplet, the continuous narration, and the servitude of imitation. Turning from Dryden to Marvell and revising the quoted line, Eliot lost a model of narrative structure, but he gained control of his poem's rhythm and tone. He did not yet have the long poem he would write, but finally he had access to its anguish and paradoxically to the more relaxed mood in which that anguish would reveal itself.

The drafts of the rest of "The Fire Sermon" show Eliot writing in short stanzas, using a first-person narrator, moving from style to style, topic to topic, until another narrative asserts itself in the typist episode with its donation of form and structure. Eliot seems to have welcomed these gifts of imitated form in the early stages of his writing as a means of sustaining a long stretch of poetry, and later, when he came to revise this section in response to Pound's frequent suggested cancellations and negative criticism, he acknowledges his gratitude to the borrowed form by suppressing the dominance of rhyme and rhythm without eliminating their force.[2]

The difference between the cancelled Fresca section and the revised typist section marks an important shift in Eliot's sense of the whole poem he was writing. At this stage, he still read it as an urban satire, still saw it in regular form based on an established model, but he had begun to handle his materials more deftly, mixing the surrealistic presence of Tiresias into the realistic scene, recasting quotations, and reducing the sarcasm.[3] He had changed his tone with the change of characters. The typist, even in the first version of this passage, has some of Fresca's pretensions, but she elicits Eliot's pity rather than his terror, and he redirects his savage attack to the man. Although Pound comments that Eliot's jabs at the man are "over the mark," clearly Eliot had found a more suitable target than Fresca in the "young man carbuncular" (CP 44).

The long poem that Eliot was composing now took on a more personal tone. The severely controlled imitation of eighteenth-century form which he apparently needed in order to start writing an extended passage gradually eased into a more open form and direct expression. Paradoxically, as he enlarged his range of references from the mock epic to the epic, he freed himself from a personal reticence that had masked itself in scorn, and the composition moved along. The next section to be written, a large part of "What the Thunder Said," was composed in one brief stretch, in contrast to the foundering composition of "The Fire Sermon."

Eliot said he was referring to his own experience with this passage when he wrote in an essay on Pascal: "It is a commonplace that some forms of illness are extremely favourable, not only to religious illumination, but to artistic and literary composition. A piece of writing meditated. [*sic*] apparently without progress for months or years, may suddenly take shape and word; and in this state long passages may be produced which require little or no retouch" (WL 129, fn. 1). Although he goes on to admit that "no masterpiece can be produced whole by such means," he does suggest that parts of it at least can be the miraculous productions of such automatic writing in which the creator has the sensation of being the vehicle of expression and not its originator.

At this point, as Kenner has pointed out, the motifs of the Grail legend began to take possession of Eliot's imagination, and perhaps these motifs proved a greater aid to composition than the model of eighteenth-century satire that Eliot had been using. It may also be that his sustained effort at composition gradually took hold of the poem. He wrote more easily because he had been writing for a longer time. Or he may suddenly have come to understand the poem he wanted to write. Much later, talking about *Four Quartets*, he admits, "That's one way in which my mind does seem to have worked throughout the years poetically—doing things separately and then seeing the possibility of fusing them together, altering them, and making a kind of whole of them." [4] Whatever the reason, it is clear that Eliot's long poem emerged in stages, the product of different conceptions of form and yet a single commitment to long form. Laboring over an imitation of Dryden, Eliot worked against himself, and yet this blockage and his persistence against it produced the delicate shifts of mood that led to the sustained work on "What the Thunder Said."

The narrative of the poem's composition must start with this last section, where Eliot first came into a sense of his poem. If, as Kenner argues, the Grail legend came to possess his imagination, then in that context a section entitled "What the Thunder Said" should be a conclusion representing the word of God. If the section seems to swerve from the expectations it arouses by its title, its opening movement at least presents what might be regarded as a preparatory scene to a final vision. Eliot is quite explicit in his footnotes about the themes employed here: the journey to Emmaus, the approach to the Chapel Perilous, the "present decay of eastern Europe" (CP 53). Although the expression of those themes becomes more fragmented and imagistic as it goes on, the narrative of the journey progresses without interruption.

Eliot is drawing here on scenes from other texts, but he is detailing them in his own voice; and there is a consistency of tone even in this fragmentation, a consistency which the earlier composition of "The Fire Sermon" had lacked. The tension builds up by repetition, "If there were water / And no rock / If there were rock / And also water," to the final disappointment, "But there is no water."[5] Then it rephrases itself in an anxious search for the identity of "the third who walks always beside you." That search also frustrated, the tension disseminates itself through the sound in the air, a general picture of civilizations in disarray that leads into the phantasmagoria of the woman fiddling on her hair. The tension becomes unbearably taut as the scene disintegrates before the empty chapel, a conventional delusion of the quester, but here all too real.

When the thunder finally speaks, all hope of communication has been abandoned, so that it speaks in a stutter from a language not known.[6] The remote language releases the poem from the immediate acknowledgment that the wastelanders are not prepared spiritually to hear what the thunder said. And even more than that, the reader is relieved of the responsibility of decoding the passage not only by the footnote which translates the *Upanishad*, but even more by someone who appears to be an obtuse respondent to the thunder, registering the thunder's commands at the lowest level.

The speaker uses the thunder's commands as an occasion for fairly continuous confession. He has not given, sympathized, or controlled, he admits, in his backward glance over his experience. And the pity is greater because he interprets the commands at a minor valuation, imagining giving as giving in to passion, "The awful daring of a moment's surrender," sympathizing as waiting for sympathy, and controlling as directing a heart as one would a boat. Suppressed within the dullness is, however, some vague awareness of a deeper meaning in the thunder's words as well as a deeper understanding of his own inadequacies as lost opportunities rather than as completely wrong turns. For example, he is aware that it is only through his surrender to passion that he has existed, only by turning the key in his prison that he has confirmed the prison, only by not inviting the heart that he has lost control of it. The respondent does understand, if dimly, the thunder's commands, despite his isolation, his ignorance, his spiritual exhaustion. But he understands them only retrospectively, and thus he will not take them as directives for the life ahead. So the thunder seems to speak in vain.

From the journey so far detailed, the quester cannot succeed, and so the interest must be all in how he fails. Eliot had at hand any number of formal and thematic possibilities, and it is interesting to see that he does not choose some of the more obvious. He resists the fragmentation of phrase, the preverbal imitative response to the stutter, and he also casts off the too insistently moralistic or, obversely, the too cynical tone. Nor does he turn to allusion and quotation. The voice that responds is direct, coherent, clear in its anguish, and yet richly cadenced, symmetrically phrased, and carefully modulated. Repetition marks its style: "By this, and this only, we have existed," "Turn in the door once and turn once only," "Gaily, to the hand expert" and

"Gaily, when invited." It is reflective, the voice of one who understands in some way the purport of the thunder's voice and the distance that separates his own experience from that voice, and yet in its measured tone it expresses perhaps too impersonally its own failure, as if it does not feel keenly the loss.

It is a strange voice, even for Eliot's many-voiced poem, and all the more so if one considers what voice could find words to speak in the presence of the thunder's words. To speak at all in response to the thunder is spiritually impossible, and yet not to speak in this poem would be to leave the poetic structure too clearly closed, as it would be left in the direct advice at the end of "Death by Water." Eliot meets this opportunity by separating the voices into different languages and rhythms. The contrast between the stutter, repeated by the listener in the fuller Sanskrit, and the conversational tone of the response marks one division between spiritual utterance and human speech. It is not simply that the speaker is isolated from the word of God, but that God speaks in forms different from rational discourse. His word must be interpreted and recast into words. He commands. His human listeners must seek to understand what he is saying through whatever means they have available. There is bound to be a shift downward in decorum from the thunder to the human voice at the same time that the voice, speaking in such exalted company, will obviously rise to its fullest expression to meet the requirements of the situation. Thus, the solemnity and measured movement of the voice are both gifts of the occasion and faults of the spirit.

In this contrast between the stuttering of the thunder's affirmative commands and the articulateness of the speaker's negative self-judgment, Eliot holds in peculiar balance the tensions of this section and ultimately of the poem. The experience which divides the quester from the thunder's voice requires definite utterance if it is not to fade away under the power of the thunder's voice. The thunder's voice will be heard in fragmented form long after the fragments of human experience have disintegrated into dust, and the recitative that Eliot sets up here acknowledges that inevitability.

In the drafts of the poem, the response to the last command of the thunder places the girl on the shore deserted by the speaker and leads directly into the lines "I sat upon the shore / Fishing" (WL 79). In the finished poem, the spaced division tends to separate the final fragments from the voice of the thunder. Such a division makes the figure here perhaps too significant symbolically; the fisher in a poem about the Fisher King will arouse immediate symbolic expectations. To connect him with the sailor who failed to control the heart of his beloved as he had his boat deflates those expectations slightly, although the movement into multiple quotations prevents any pursuit of either meaning.

The heap of broken quotations with which Eliot ends his poem suggests that we can know nothing. Structures are crumbling all about the figure who asks about order. The disarray is total as Eliot rushes to conclusion by repeating what the thunder said in Sanskrit and offering the benediction "Shantih shantih shantih." Here working at cross-purposes and under severe tension is one voice of a poet who wants to shore up the ruins of the poem by offering an interpretative order and another voice of a poet whose fertile and well-stocked memory casts up one quotation after another to delay any conclusion. The first voice forces the final lines on a poem which has just demonstrated that peace, if it is to come, will pass all understanding possible in this world.

In the discontinuity of the ending, which Eliot wrote in an intermediary stage of the compositional process and not as the summary of an already finished poem, he has discovered the use of the double voice which would come to dominate the revisions of earlier sections. If the person speaking in this section is the person who has listened to what the thunder said, the disorientation of the passage may be attributed to the withdrawal of the thunder and the return to a familiar world now made bafflingly unfamiliar. In such a state, snatches of lines he has read pass through his mind made newly vacant by the departure of the thunder's voice. The ruins on which these quotations focus offer a surrealistic display of the end of the world. Yet this passage, in its confusion and disorder, drives the auditor of the thunder's words to redouble his efforts toward control. The world he had known has just been destroyed, and the world he is to know has not been created. Torn between them, he can try to resume some rational program, set his lands in order, or shore fragments against his ruin, even as he feels the pressures operating against just such a task.

Eliot turns to quotation here perhaps out of a reluctance to formulate an ending. The fragments themselves point to the inconclusiveness of any ending: Arnaut Daniel's speaking from hell, Philomel and Procne's transformation, the dead and repeatedly dying Prince D'Aquitaine, Hieronymo's revenge play. These references all indicate an end beyond the ending. The character of the mad and maddened poet recurs here in these fragments as a final effort to resist the formal finish of the poem. Eliot cannot simply have fertility and order restored to a section that has constantly restricted itself to chaos and sterility. And, of course, when this section came to conclude the poem, the pressure against resolution intensified. At the same time, if the Grail legend to which Eliot refers here is not to be simply superfluous in the modern world, its force must be felt in some way. If the thunder's voice is to be taken seriously, even in its failed articulation, then it must leave all speech in some way affected. Here, it divides the lines, it breaks up the sense, it reestablishes the ruins even as they are being shored up. And once its energies have worked, the voice returns to reiterate its commands and to offer in its formal ending the benediction to the faithful. The consolation is brief and in a language unknown to its auditors, but across these immense gaps it makes itself heard in complete form.[7] The penultimate line may repeat what the thunder said and so close off any understanding of its riddle, but as the last

voice we hear it has the authority of its place at what will become the end of a long poem.

This ending dramatizes in brief the way Eliot took the plan of
the Grail legend first into this section of the poem and then into
the longer poem it was to end. Weston had assured him that the
Grail legend would never die, that after slumbering for centuries
it had reawakened through the genius of Wagner and Tennyson.[8]
By attempting to write about the present day, Eliot set himself a
task more difficult than those assumed by these nineteenth-
century artists. He was not going to restore the myths by writing
of King Arthur's court, but rather by writing about modern London. For that purpose, he had to accommodate the discontinuity
and disorganization of modern life within the larger structure of
the continuous myth. He had to suggest that the Grail symbols
were nowhere apparent in this world, and at the same time he
had to find them in the most unlikely places. He had to express
the spiritual aridity of the times and leave open the possibility of
the spirit's fructifying energies. He had to point to the wrong
way (Madame Sosostris') and hint at the right way. But chiefly
he had to find some means of suggesting that the conditions of
the modern world were susceptible to the workings of the spirit,
while holding in abeyance the sure presence of faith. He had to
balance the continuity of the legend with what appeared to be
the discontinuity of modern life. And above all, he had to keep
the poetry alive around and through and within the interpretation of life it might offer.

This poetic structure teeters always on the precarious balance
between the immense discontinuities of its lines and the rigor-
ous continuity of the fertility myth, between the poet's anarchic
creative energies and the anthropologist's organizing schemes,
between the immediacy of chaos and the remote hope of order.
Such a shaky structure was reinforced by Eliot's late appeal to
the anthropologists. Not only does the poem's syncretic method
parallel that of the anthropological textbook, but Weston's plan
itself must be made to emerge from the poem's welter of evi-

dence. At the same time, a poem that attempts to rely on anthropological findings will differ from a textbook by its evocative power. It will make real rather than argue its case, and its power will rest in its language and not in its documentary evidence. There will be then of necessity a resistance in the poetic text to stating its purposes directly even when the plan drawn from anthropology intrudes itself.

Finally, the poet who finds the plan of his poem in anthropology assumes in part the scientist's skepticism toward the plan. All evidence is possible proof; all evidence is possibly irrelevant. The purpose that Weston's book provided for Eliot was double-edged. It allowed him to structure a long poem, to break into that structure, to reform it, and go on. The discontinuities which it permitted and encouraged made the continuity of long form possible for Eliot. It provided an acceptable scaffolding behind which Eliot could explore the variety of his creative anxieties. Because anthropological conclusions are something he did not have to *believe* in, Eliot could use them as he willed, pointing to clear evidence of Weston's symbolism in the modern world and just as quickly erasing that significance. The poem moves toward and away from Weston's plan, developing in its refusal to follow a straight and continuous line of development.

If there is no principle of generation in the wasteland, correspondingly there is no plan of growth in the poem. Roots do not clutch and grow, nothing connects with nothing, even language itself disintegrates. Similarly, sections of the poem trail into quotations, break off and take up again a new subject; one speaker neither listens to nor hears another, hordes of people enter and depart to little purpose. It is in this randomness, however, this giving off of energy, this breaking down and discontinuity, that the poem goes on. In this respect, Eliot's writing is not like the mythological method of Joyce that Eliot so admired.[9] Where Joyce sets up parallels between ancient times and modern, Eliot breaks down any consistent parallel in order to present conflicting evidence, to suggest difficulties, to test possibilities, and in the process to reveal his initiating inventiveness and energy.

In completing "What the Thunder Said," Eliot had devised a method of composition and a structure for his poem. He then began to reconceive the entire poem, parts of which he had written with a different model in mind. He cut and revised these parts on his own and following Pound's suggestions, but he did not start over again from the beginning. Kenner calls the finished poem "a form with no form, and a genre with no name," although in this respect it is not unlike other long poems, for example, *Paradise Lost* or *The Prelude*.[10]

The form of *The Waste Land* is both complex and difficult to comprehend because the poem was conceived and composed under difficult and varying circumstances. The whole poem Eliot had in mind to write changed as he wrote the parts, changed with the parts, but the parts too had to be changed in the final reworking of the poem. Willing to reconceive the long poem, graft new reconceptions on old parts, and even to let the poem take shape and work suddenly without conscious intervention, Eliot forced the poem he had originally had in mind to write to contend with the poem he finally put on paper. The discontinuities between the two reflect discontinuities in the inspiration and composition of the poem, both overcome finally by the consistently more forceful and triumphant idea of a continuous long poem.

Once he had composed "What the Thunder Said," Eliot assembled the drafts of the sections he had written and showed them to Pound. Working with Pound's suggestions and with his own reconsideration of the poem, he then went back to revise extensively the various sections he had accumulated in a random process of composition. The parts were entitled "He Do the Police in Different Voices (1): Part 1," "He Do the Police in Different Voices: Part II," "The Fire Sermon" (unnumbered), and "Part IV: Death by Water." This numbering of the parts established their final order, and in revising them, Eliot did not change this first ordering of the parts or the discreteness of each part. Nor did Pound's editorial comments suggest any reorganization of the poem's sectional divisions. Thus, Eliot settled on the large outline of the poem, the drafted sections of which were in shambles. Destroying the heroic stanza that had carried long stretches of his work and abandoning the urban satire as a central mode, Eliot replaced these organizing principles with another means of formal control by simply numbering the poem's sections. From this point on, the order in which the sections were written was superseded by the order in which they were now placed and within which they were revised. It is not surprising that the long poem offered some resistance to its revision and that its final form is a compromise between the sections, which were written as parts of a long poem still to be conceptualized, and the whole, which was imagined at some intermediary stage after the sections had taken on an independent identity.

The new and relatively commodious organization that emerged in the composition of "What the Thunder Said" allowed Eliot great latitude in his efforts to revise the sections he had in first draft. He had, however, to redirect them toward the end he now envisioned. This program carried him through the radical revisions and eventual publication of the poem, but the passion for form that drove Eliot to imitate Pope and admire Dryden in the early stages of work on *The Waste Land* was not fully satiated in this method of composition. It surfaced again when he lengthened the poem for publication as a book by adding the footnotes. He may have added the notes simply to add pages to the poem, but once more he tried to impose a plan, and again he dallied with its attractions, setting it up and dismantling it simultaneously.

Presumably if he had taken the plan of the poem from *From Ritual to Romance*, he would have had difficulty neither in charting the poem nor in appending the footnotes. But, like the poem itself, the footnotes pursue their independent and somewhat dilatory way. Often they point to passages in other texts that strike Eliot's interests as being quite independent from those of *The Waste Land*. Or, characteristically, they start with an admission of ignorance: "I am not familiar with the exact constitution of the Tarot pack," "I do not know the origin of the ballad," "This may not appear as exact as Sappho's line." In these notes, Eliot seems to hold off as well as point to his sources. The text itself shifts and wobbles, and never more so than in its attempts to establish a relationship to its source material. Eliot toys with plans in these footnotes in much the same way that his poem puts itself together and then pulls apart, resisting any final closure. When Eliot admits in a headnote that his poem is difficult, he articulates his own difficulties with the text, his disinclination to settle on any plan even as he desired one, and a perverse willingness to break into every continuity he could establish.

Eliot's attitude toward his own poem's lengthy development leads to a peculiar strategy according to which he veers between simple and direct efforts to state the poem's point quite explicitly—"Fear death by water," "I Tiresias have foresuffered all," "Consider Phlebas," "We who were living are now dying"—and an evasion of all such direct statements. The unavoidable continuity of the vegetation myths which, Eliot claimed late in its composition, underpinned the poem, is severely tested by the discontinuity of the text, the one dependent on the other if the poem is to develop beyond loosely joined fragments. As it was put into final form, the poem gained its length through an antagonistic struggle between an internal tendency toward discontinuity and a rigid plan for continuity imposed late and tentatively.

The continuity of the vegetation myths and the attempt to indicate the continuity of the text in the footnotes are external efforts to shore up the poem and lengthen it. In the final reworking of the poem, Eliot made some effort to add to the poem itself internal pointers toward its larger conception. The voice of the explicator may be heard throughout the poem explaining and justifying its radically new artistic process. But also apparent throughout the poem is another voice, rescuing the mystery of creation from too plain explication by starting over again in another place. Both the narrative of composition and the narrative of the poem develop in this dialogue between the poet's two voices. Pound, despite his own proclivities for explanation, urged Eliot to suppress the explicator, although some of the cuts and revisions of the drafts actually work to focus the overt explicator.

Yet, both in the writing and in the revision, Eliot seemed to respond to an internal dialogue between the poet as experimenter and the poet as explicator. Throughout the poem, after some bafflingly original poetic passage, the explicator will emerge to point the moral, reduce the novelty, impose an often fairly tedious order. For example, after the surrealistic encounter between Stetson and his interlocutor at the end of the "The Burial of the Dead," the explicator concludes, " 'You! hypocrite lecteur!—mon semblable,—mon frère!'" In French and a quotation from Baudelaire, the line informs us by this circuitous route that if we have been confused by the confusion of levels of language and of reality in the preceding passage, we are implicated nonetheless simply by reading, in this confusion, the process by which the banal turns ominous and the accustomed turns strange. The strangeness of the text is held off by this acknowledgment of fraternity, as we are made to share the precariousness of language, the tentativeness of reality, with the poet.

Explicator and creator can also change voice, and this passage is a good example of such possibilities for reversal. The talk of Mylae, of corpses planted, and of the enigmatic Dog, in a tedious conversation of chance greeting between two old army acquaintances, would seem to indicate a desire on the speaker's part to see his life and activity as unified by larger rhythms and references, to imagine himself as participating in significant rituals.[11] If this wish to explain expresses the speaker's effort to impose a larger unity on the poem as well as on his own activity, then we may imagine that the voice which interrupts his conversations by quoting Baudelaire is that of the poet, reminding us of our voyeurism while establishing the strangeness of the passage.

At points, and especially in those parts composed first, the poem casts up particular moments that pull against any imposition of order. For example, lines 186 to 202 of "The Fire Sermon"—where references to urban waste mix with quotations from *The Tempest*, the Australian ballad, the line from *Parsifal*—defy in their elaborate overlay of details any organizing principle. The associations can perhaps be followed: the rat on the bank calls up the canal which suggests the fishing; the fishing restores the idea of the Fisher King, who brings up other dead or impotent kings as in *The Tempest*, and then there is a break in the associations made by a slash of visual detail, an image of white bodies and bones. This mention moves the poem back to the earlier reference from Marvell concerning time's erosion of the desirable body, and Marvell perhaps recalls John Day; and once the poem moves into songs, the ballad of Mrs. Porter comes to mind, followed by singing voices from *Parsifal*, which dwindle finally into the pre-verbal song of the nightingale, "Twit twit twit." But the passage as a whole escapes any sense of its inevitability.

One of the passages written earliest in the poem, this section seems to move in two or three directions. The ironic contrast between Mrs. Porter's ballad and the children singing in *Parsifal* places Mrs. Porter's lust in opposition to the purity both of the children and the Grail knight. In addition, Eliot has fixed the references to the Fisher King and the Grail legend in a setting of modern urban squalor to force another contrast, pointing to the hopelessness of redemption in the modern world. But there are also countermovements to that logic: the original fishing, the lovemaking, and the washing of the feet are all spring rites, and if their form is possible in the modern world, perhaps their value might be restored, so that there is the possibility of continuity as well as discontinuity here. More than that, there is a certain phantasmagoric quality about this scene which counterpoints its realism and blurs the whole picture: the rat is creeping through the vegetation in the winter and the protagonist is fishing in the evening, thus disturbing the seasonal and diurnal rhythms that have been so pointedly established.

Unless the poem is simply self-cancelling, the movement and countermovement, clearing and blurring of images, and reversible points of view indicate a double purpose or a willful disunity in the verse. The passage expresses a repugnance at filth, at waste, at sexuality, at the same time that it suggests the hope that something of value will come out of these conditions, as it did for Ferdinand, for Parsifal, for Philomel, all figures of loss recuperated. Satire mixes with a kind of suppressed prayer here to express the public doubt, the private hope. The role that the quotations play is to double the doubleness, to impose an interpretation on an interpretation, to elicit a public or documented hope from the private doubt.

But the passage finally resists cohesion, and the pressure point of resistance is in those lines which break the fisher's reverie: "White bodies naked on the low damp ground / And bones cast in a little low dry garret." They pick up an earlier reference to rattling bones in line 186, bring to the front of the mind the figure of death, curtail the musing, insist on littleness and lowness. They divide the muser from the luster, and their purpose may be in their divisiveness, the barrier they throw up to narrative or thematic continuity, the indications they give of subterranean powers beneath the full control of the referential force at the surface of the text. This section was put together early, rearranged, radically cut, and revised. That it still retains its uncertainty of purpose despite its reworking points to a tenacious strand in the narrative of composition. Eliot's basic attention was to the line or the limited unit of lines, not to the longer form. He *borrowed* a system of continuity; he *created* by discontinuous sections.

Eliot's genius, manifest both as he composed the poem and as he put it together finally for publication, inheres in his sensitivity to many voices and to mutually contradictory impulses even as he longed for a structure that would reconcile them. In one sense, if Jessie L. Weston and Sir James Frazer are correct, there can be no escaping the larger and more general rhythms of belief; the accidents of culture and of time can all be accommodated in these vast systematizing projects. Thus the chaos of the modern world that overwhelms Eliot must be imagined as merely apparent. Beneath its surface moves the same seasonal continuity which produced the vegetative myths and which can again restore meaning. Yet such assurance is nowhere available to the poet.

Eliot's reconception of the poem was in his mind when he revised "The Burial of the Dead" to open with *April*, and the multiple voices this opening introduces both echo the voices of "What the Thunder Said" and establish the countercurrents that will run through the poem. There is first the voice of the commentator who possesses at the start an interpretation of seasonal changes, or rather resists the interpretation that might suggest there is any meaning to the lilacs spring breeds. But a different voice breaks through his weariness and despair with the idea that "Summer surprised us," particularizing the moment and redeeming it from easy interpretation. There is a kind of eagerness in the speaker's introduction of herself (however muted by its expression in German) and in her willingness to communicate even her most deep-seated fears.

Still, the opportunities of the moment are thwarted, and the possible redemption of both the time and the season falters. The voice of the commentator returns to ask, "What are the roots that clutch, what branches grow / Out of this stony rubbish?" This relatively short opening announces the persistent way in which the poem will develop—one voice interrupting the next voice, cancelling it out briefly, and in turn being silenced. No dialogue develops, no story continues, no commentary concludes. In fact, fragmentation rather than finish assures continuity.

The poem seems to proceed casually until the commentator moves in the next sentence to say, "Son of man, / You cannot say, or guess, for you know only / A heap of broken images." Here he reveals his purposes too sharply. The biblical terms here, "Son of man," the cricket, the red rock, fear in a handful of dust, seem to stop the poem, remove it from the Hofgarten scene, elevate it too quickly to some generalized significance or arena of failed significance. In the drafts, this section is marked off by asterisks as if it were to be self-contained, and the lines actually have their genesis in a poem written as early as 1915, "The Death of St. Narcissus." Here, as an interruption of the narrative scene, they must be read in some way as a comment on that scene, and indeed when the narrative continues after the song from *Tristan and Isolde*, it seems to have picked up some of the fear and brokenness of that passage. The girl here may be the girl in the earlier scene, now shadowed by some ominous foreboding perhaps emanating from this bodiless voice.

The poem shifts its focus altogether with the introduction of Madame Sosostris, who manages to interject the major motifs of the poem, as Eliot too candidly explains in the footnotes, marking all the connections between the Tarot and Frazer and the various sections of the poem that had been written. A poem in which the symbols are so blatantly stated is under the necessity either of making them work directly by allegory or of diverting attention from them while they work indirectly. In choosing the second possibility, Eliot also offers a countermovement of realism to the simple imposition of symbolic significance through Madame Sosostris' cards. The "Unreal city" is all too real, and the vignette of city crowds seems to cancel out the warnings of the fortune-teller by dark hints of its total meaninglessness. The two movements—toward a depthless reality *and* a submerged meaning—are brought together in the conversation with Stetson. Thus the first section comes to a climax in which the overt symbolism is smothered by covert realism.

The second section of *The Waste Land* swerves widely from the symbols and themes introduced in "The Burial of the Dead." Yet even here there emerge, although faintly, some details that throw the whole scene into disarray. For example, the picture of Philomel over the mantel of this luxuriously described room might have been in accord with the other details of conspicuous consumption and a slightly decadent taste were it not for the lines "yet there the nightingale / Filled all the desert with inviolable voice." *There* is set in opposition to here, and thus we are reminded of a parallel between here and there, between the present world and that other world of inviolable values. The explicator in the poet steps forward to point out "other withered stumps of time" and to underscore the purpose of the details. Almost immediately, as if again the directives have been too explicit, the scene turns surrealistic or macabre, and the woman at her dressing table is imagined as a witch with hair "Spread out in fiery points." Then the spaced interval and the turn into conversation mark another quick diversion from the forward thrust of the interpreter.

But the easily interrupted conversation reveals in its discontinuity a continuity in the symbolism, as narrative and symbol play off against each other throughout the section. The speaker remembers "pearls that were his eyes," recapitulating references to death by water, in answer to the woman's frantic questioning, "'Do you remember / Nothing?'" As the conversation switches social levels and moves into the pub, the habit continues. The publican's interruption, "HURRY UP PLEASE ITS TIME," sets the scene for Lil's friend, but it also announces the major symbolic structure of this section.

That Eliot was working toward a greater continuity in his poem as he revised is suggested by the opening of "The Fire Sermon," where the opening river goes back through Ophelia to London Bridge to Madame Sosostris' warning of death by water in a leisurely circuit through the poem. These opening lines were a late revision of this section. Eliot worked through various versions of the Fresca opening before cancelling it entirely and replacing it with this section, lines that were first simply sketched in pencil on the back of the finished Fresca manuscript. But the promise of the opening phrase—"The river's tent is broken"—with its suggestion of spring rains, the sound of water, which might pick up a motif from the superimposed Grail legend, is immediately undercut by mysterious indications that it is not spring and yet not any other season either. The "last fingers of leaf" might indicate fall except, as "The wind / Crosses the brown land," it may be late winter or some time out of the seasons in a mythical land permanently parched. Then the ominous connotations of the words present themselves: the river's tent is broken and thus becomes another broken image to add to the poem's heap.

A later addition to the section is the Psalmist's lamentation, "By the waters of Leman I sat down and wept," which expresses the weariness of the poet in the face of the task that presents itself to him. Again, like the Psalmist, the poet too weeps not simply from despair but out of a sense of indignation at the scene he witnesses. The modern "nymphs" and "their friends, the loitering heirs of city directors," comport themselves in a manner that saddens the poet, rouses his instinct for satirical denigration, and yet somehow paralyzes his will to go on. This sentiment is absent from the earliest drafts and may have been imposed by a poet who has himself grown weary with his composition and the subject that seems to have overtaken it.

This section is awash with quotations, half-formed references, uncompleted allusions. Especially as a contrast to the previous section and its narrative continuity, "The Fire Sermon" seems excessively discontinuous, or rather so inclusive as to be entirely random. These two qualities flow into each other when the section moves away from its one extended and coherent scene in the typist's room into a flood of music. The references are multiple: Ariel's dirge from *The Tempest*, the Rhine-daughters from *Götterdämmerung* as the Thames-daughters, descriptions of Queen Elizabeth sporting with Leicester on the barge, the *Purgatorio*, St. Augustine's *Confessions*, Buddha's *Fire Sermon*. The organizing principle of this particular group of allusions is difficult to detect, and the context of the poem, so weakened here by the welter of extratextual references, cannot do much to unite them.

Eliot's need to bolster his text by elaborate use of allusions might come from a simple unwillingness to formulate a direct expression of the theme of lust. When he is handling the theme satirically, as in the typist scene, he can be quite clear, realistic, and relatively nonallusive. In that passage as well, he exerts a kind of rigid control through the formality of the verse, the resurgence of a rhyme scheme, the embedded sonnet form. Once that control of form and tone gives way, however, the lines break, the moods swing, and the allusions multiply. The divisiveness of the text here seems to erupt from some generating division of purpose in the poet himself. Exactly what attitude the poem would take toward the lust of "The Fire Sermon" remains unclear. The satirical treatment of the typist would be one possible response, the lament of the Psalmist another, and still another would be the faith of St. Augustine.

Eliot's fascination with lust, as well as his ambivalence, continue in the early version of the next section, "Death by Water," as Eliot opens with a vignette of the sailor's "comic gonorrhea" (WL 55). Had this section been allowed to stand in the poem as written and as placed after the original version of "The Fire Sermon," it would have added an extraneous narrative dimension. Eliot's apparent doubts about the section, compounded by Pound's summary statement that it was "Bad," forced him to consider abandoning it entirely. Instead, he followed Pound's advice and reduced it drastically because Pound felt it was in its brevity as necessary as in its length it was superfluous. After

"The Fire Sermon," even the section's allusiveness seems clear. But references to Phoenicians, to death by water, to Gentiles and Jews, crowd together in a density that is not necessarily fully meaningful. Still, the final lines, "O you who turn the wheel and look to windward, / Consider Phlebas, who was once handsome and tall as you," are so direct and pointed that the riddle of the earlier lines may be simply overlooked. Here, the critic comes to the front of the poem to interpret its meaning.

As Ezra Pound noted, the section is needed because it recovers the reference to the drowned Phoenician in Madame Sosostris' pack of cards, and so it serves as a pointer in the symbolic development of the poem. Stripped as it is here to its bare bones, the section is perhaps too skeletal, too merely useful as a point of direction, although Eliot covers this bareness somewhat by such random facts as the whispering current under the sea, stages of his life through which Phlebas passes in death, the whirlpool he enters. Like the bones in the low garret and the woman with hair spread in fiery points, the details of Phlebas' death are puzzling reminders that we do not really know where we are or what fate awaits us, that even the poet seems uncertain.

At the same time, the direct warning at the end of "Death by Water" points to a promise in the title of the final section, "What the Thunder Said," and prepares for a conclusion. As we have seen, the inspiration that allowed Eliot to write that section in one brief stretch did not emerge from a clear sense of its place as the summary of a long poem. Rather, it came from a fascination with the motifs of the Grail legend that had little relevance to the urban satire he had been writing. Long after the inspiration of "What the Thunder Said" had flagged, Eliot revised the poem's earlier sections in the light of this final section, but "What the Thunder Said" still retains the energy of its original composition as a different kind of poem from the sections Eliot had been composing. If this section were separated from the earlier sections, it might be read as the first stage of Eliot's movement from satire to meditative poetry. But as the conclusion of *The Waste Land*, it must be misread as the end of the quest which started with *April*.

The narrative of *The Waste Land*'s composition is unique in the history of literature, not only because of the way one major poet allowed another major poet to revise and reform a long work, but more significantly because of the way one poet put together an assortment of drafts, written at different times and in different styles, into a final long poem. This narrative suggests something about both the tenacity and the inadequacy of the Modernist imagination as it confronted the dilemma of long form. It has been argued that Eliot composed in short lyrics which he eventually put together in a longer form or that he learned to put together a long poem by a spatial arrangement in which one short poem could be visualized as linked to another. This narrative of composition should suggest that, while Eliot did compose in short units, he was driven to write by a desire for the long form. The sections that he wrote may have been brief and disconnected, but he had in mind from the beginning a long poem into which they would be placed. It was not their spatial form that taught him how to put them together, since he composed them not in the sequence in which they were published but in a random sequence from which they were finally wrenched into final form.

Eliot was the first of the Modernist poets to long for long form. He had no means of imagining it. In the course of writing a satire, he came to rely on an external form borrowed from the cultural anthropologists which allowed him to express himself more freely than the external poetic form he had borrowed from the eighteenth-century satirists. So he revised a poem he had been writing according to one model by layering over it another model, still leaving parts of the original model in place. The result is a peculiar form that is held together by the tension between its discontinuous parts and a rigorously continuous but extraneous narrative pattern.

As the first long poem of the Modernist movement, *The Waste Land* set the style and encouraged Eliot's contemporaries to contest its preeminence. It also established a method of composition that Eliot was to repeat in later long poems. The creation of a single long poem out of parts conceived and written as separate sections or isolated poems became a persistent pattern in Eliot's career and suggests the extent to which the idea of the long poem emerged in his imagination out of the creative process itself. Unlike the ancient writers of long poems he so admired, Eliot himself did not attempt to write an epic. Clearly, however, he was not only responsive to the long form that came to him, but consistently eager for some form beyond the short lyric poem even if he lacked the resources to imagine it at the beginning. Toward the end of his career, he lamented "Twenty years largely wasted," "Trying to learn to use words, and every attempt / Is a wholly new start, and a different kind of failure." He acknowledges here not only his long career and the long wastage in that career, but also the tenacity of words and of forms that failures create.

The example of Eliot's effort in the composition of *The Waste Land* was not wasted on his contemporaries. Crane, Williams, and Pound saw in that poem an accomplishment that they would have to rival. They may have misunderstood the poem, and they may have inaccurately set themselves in opposition to it; but they saw in it the triumph of long form that made the short lyrics they had been writing suddenly inadequate responses to the modern world. *The Waste Land* moved them to a new stage of creativity. Overlooking Eliot's difficulties with long form and largely ignorant of the stages through which he had worked to compose his poem, these poets began to consider the long form. They started in different places and worked toward different ends, but they all began to search for an outline, a projected structure that would support sustained composition. At the same time, they began to write short sections of the projected long poem, and their long poems emerged gradually in this tension between the conception of the whole and the creation of the parts. As with *The Waste Land*, the parts of these long poems are both independent of the projected larger structures and paradoxically dependent on them. The narratives of the compositions of *The Bridge, Paterson,* and *The Cantos* are more protracted than that of *The Waste Land*; but they bear a strange resemblance to it.

3 The Bridge

IT IS HAZARDOUS to begin writing a long poem at the end, and all the more so with a long poem that will rely on the poet's moments of inspiration. Hart Crane's difficulties in writing *The Bridge* may be traced to this peculiar method of composition and to the assumptions about form that it embodies. Crane finished the final section of *The Bridge* first, and he called it "Atlantis." With that section completed, it was hard to begin the poem, harder still because Crane saw the ending as "symphonic in including the convergence of all the strands separately detailed in antecedent sections of the poem—Columbus, conquests of water, land, etc., Pokahantus, subways, offices, etc., etc." (LHC 232). To begin at the end, where Poe thought all works of art should begin, placed almost insurmountable restrictions on the unwritten long poem; and Crane's completion of "Atlantis," a poem on which he had been working for three years, brought his writing on *The Bridge* to a temporary halt. "Atlantis" was the ending for a beginning that Crane could not imagine, and when he recommenced work on the long poem again some months later, he wrote a poem that essentially recasts "Atlantis"—"To Brooklyn Bridge." Then his writing stopped again. Eventually he resumed work on the poem, and, hedged in by a beginning balanced and doubled by the ending, Crane in one summer wrote most of the intervening sections.

In a different way from Eliot, Crane started his long poem too early, before he had prepared himself to write it. He imagined both that the long poem would come to him and that he could block it out first. He prepared an outline of the poem, and *The Bridge* emerged from a struggle between its inspired moments of composition and a preliminary plan. The plan proved to be an obstruction as well as an aid, encouraging creation but encouraging also the insights that made the plan unworkable. This long poem has always posed the problem of its organizational principle. If *The Waste Land* suffered from a dilatory composition and a structure realized only in the middle of the composition, *The Bridge* may suggest the problems presented by a plan developed fully prior to composition. The composition of *The Bridge* suggests that a predetermined structure can restrain the clarity of expression it is designed to serve.[1]

Crane's peculiarly deterministic method of writing reveals an uncertainty about the long form and an anxiety about how to channel his creative impetuosity into a sustained work. These fears he attempted to allay by methods that were destined to intensify them. But this narrative of composition also indicates the importance of such antagonistic creative habits. *The Bridge* develops by evading its supposed purposes.

It is not surprising, then, that the poem has always appeared to be a structural puzzle. Crane's first critics judged the poem brilliant in parts but inadequate as a total work. Later readers found the poem as a whole sturdy, but identified some sections as weak. Still later, the failure or success of the larger structure was seen as of one piece with the failure or success of the individual sections. One critic has argued that "Crane's long poems do not develop, they recur," and the problems of organization that such a "poetics of failure" requires manifest themselves both in the part and in the whole.[2] Thus, questions of organization—always the first and most crucial points of debate for a long poem—have tended to force the very judgment from which they have arisen.

Actually, Crane himself was his first negative critic. Even before he had written anything but the ending of *The Bridge*, he began to suspect that he would not be able to construct the long poem, not because his own creative powers were inadequate, but because he could find no material on which to exercise them. It is a curious complaint for a poet committed to inspiration and to art as creation rather than imitation. Still, he commented, "intellectually judged the whole theme and project seems more and more absurd." And he goes on to say: "The symbols of reality necessary to articulate the span—may not exist where you expected them, however. By which I mean that however great their subjective significance to me is concerned—these forms, materials, dynamics are simply non-existent in the world" (LHC 261). And once he had finished the poem, he admitted to Allen Tate, "My vision of poetry *is* too personal to 'answer the call'" (LHC 353).

His sense of failure, early and late, stemmed from what he imagined was a failure of vision. Like Pound, Crane judged himself by his ability to see a unified meaning within the fragments of history. For him, the poem was to be a vision of synthesis or wholeness: "a mystical synthesis of 'America,'" "a symbol of consciousness, knowledge, spiritual unity," the "Myth of America" (LHC 124, 241, 305). And like Pound too, he underestimated the power of his creative strength to vindicate history by revising it. But his stated ambition toward a synthesis is much more conservative than the poem he actually wrote. His aspirations here call for a fixed form that was always at odds both with the proliferation of material on which it was imposed and with his own febrile creative energy.

Starting at the end became a persistent strategy by which Crane could satisfy his need for synthesis, and at the same time give free expression to a creative resistance to closure. The poem as a whole, its sections, and even its lines appear consistently to start at the end. For example, the final section, "Atlantis," opens with a vision of the whole bridge ("bound cable strands, the arching path") and a vision of wholeness ("Sibylline voices flicker, waveringly stream / As though a god were issue of the strings. . . ."). It ends at the beginning with that vision just about to be accomplished ("the orphic strings, / Sidereal phalanxes, leap and converge") and with a questioning of vision ("Is it Cathay, / Now pity steeps the grass and rainbows ring / The serpent with the eagle in the leaves. . . ?"). Stanza after stanza opens with an image of wholeness and moves to more tentative images: "bound cable strands" and "voices flicker," "hails, farewells" and "splintered in the straits," "Swift peal of secular light" and "harvests in sweet torment," "thine Everpresence" and "Whispers antiphonal." Even individual lines open and end in that way: "One arc synoptic of all tides below," "In single chrysalis the many twain," "O Answerer of all,—Anemone." The synopsis, singleness, answer, must be inevitably broken down into parts.

This poem and the larger poem which it launched develop neither by "symphonic convergence," nor by synthesis, nor by unifying strands. Both "Atlantis" and *The Bridge* set out an image of completion or wholeness, and then proceed to break it down. This method operates at every level of the poem, from section to stanza to line to word combinations. Typically, the most complete form precedes its parts, and the parts, once they are enumerated, do not fit neatly together as a whole. Despite Crane's desire to affirm and unify, his poem tends to question and disassemble.

Crane's visionary inclinations, what R. W. B. Lewis has called

his "apocalyptic *hope*,"³ are usually cited as reasons for the discrepancy between the poem he imagined and the one he actually was able to write. As his comments to Frank that are quoted
above suggest, when Crane despaired he seemed to despair of
constructing the bridge between the real world and his image of
it, of finding materials to embody his vision. Yet, the actual narrative of composition as well as the poem that emerged from it
do not support this view.

Almost from the beginning and certainly as soon as he had
completed "Atlantis," Crane had a sense of the whole poem and
the experiences that would form it. In an early letter to his bene-
factor, Otto Kahn, he laid out the sections that were to comprise
The Bridge which, with the exception of the John Brown part
and the two sections written last, he then proceeded to write.
He had the evidence from history already sorted out, and he
had also clearly established the symbolic significance of figures
such as Columbus and Pocahontas. Nor were modern examples
lacking from this early summary. He could already identify the
subway section as "a kind of purgatory in relation to the open
sky of last section" (LHC 241). There may be a certain visionary
element in this outline, even a naive optimism about the creative process that lay ahead, but this scaffolding of the poem
does not indicate a mind anxious for material to embody an
idea. Nor was Crane misled about the symbolic significance of
any element in the projected poem. Here, as in the finished
poem, Pocahontas stands for "the natural body of America-
fertility," and Columbus and Whitman are likewise accurately
identified (LHC 241).

It might be argued that Crane's poem had been overdetermined, too clearly thought out before it was written through.
But his difficulties in actually writing the poem would suggest
otherwise. He composed in fits of inspiration that were in some
minor way controlled by the plan, threatening to subvert its
dominance and yet dependent on it too. For example, the climax of "Atlantis" is suspended at the end, but *The Bridge* does

not develop by careful stages of increasing intensity up to this poem, which Crane described as a "sweeping dithyramb in which the Bridge becomes the symbol of consciousness spanning time and space" (LHC 241). Nor is there any gradual movement toward that ending. Sections do not build on one another; individual sections do not work toward affirmative conclusions. Yet the movement is not aleatory, because the composition appears to depend on this initiating structure which was there to encourage the poet when his inspiration flagged. Crane struggled through vision and revision to write a long poem that would fit between the ecstatic ending and beginning that, in their finish, offered no principle of development except the possibility that they could be repeated, dismantled, or recreated.

The ambition to project a long poem was fixed by the poet's fear of inadequacy, which inspired a too elaborate conception of the task ahead; this in turn created a failure of expression, so that Crane was always working at odds with himself. He explained his method to Kahn: "Naturally I am encountering many unexpected formal difficulties in satisfying my conception, especially as one's original idea has a way of enlarging steadily under the spur of daily concentration on minute details of execution" (LHC 241). The discrepancy is between the whole and the parts, between the colossal conception of wholeness, completion, and ending, and the proliferating parts needed to make up that idea. But, as the narrative of the poem's composition reveals, Crane made the middle sections of the poem not only difficult to write but impossible even as an experiment in composition. Every section had to be wedged between the unity of beginning and end. Each part would threaten the whole and keep open the hazards of long form, even as the poem lengthened out. No bridges, the sections of *The Bridge* deny their connective functions as they vie for autonomy within the poem's larger structure.

This process of development differentiates *The Bridge* from most poems which gain their length from some generative process. Because Crane starts his poem with a finished structure, the Brooklyn Bridge, "Answerer of all," "Atlantis," he has no way of generating a poem. Even when the poem undoes its end and moves toward origins, it either appropriates them or it denies their validity, destroying not only the idea of progress but the possibility of long form. For example, in the actual image of the bridge, Crane hears "labyrinthine mouths of history / Pouring reply," "Jason! hesting Shout!," "Beams yelling Aeolus," all voices from antiquity still present in the bridge, which is then identified as "O Choir, translating time." Thus, mythic origins are incorporated into the technological end, not superseded by it. At other points in "Atlantis," Crane seems anxious to envision the end as obviating or excusing the beginning, as he says:

Migrations that must needs void memory,
Inventions that cobblestone the heart,—
Unspeakable Thou Bridge to Thee, O Love.
Thy pardon for this history, whitest Flower.

To conceive of the bridge in these two ways is to make links with the past either unnecessary or impossible, and in either case it prevents any poetic development based on generation. In order to write a long poem at all from this beginning, Crane had to keep repeating the ending, enlarging it with details, as he said, in a process which might be called degenerative form. He did not work toward wholeness and completion, but rather away from them, toward endlessly proliferating parts.

Crane's problems with form, which appear to derive from a too rigidly and extravagantly conceived whole, have their origin in his early uncertainty about representation. The drafts of "Atlantis" suggest that Crane wanted to represent the bridge as evidence of wholeness in the broken modern world, but he had not decided whether meaning inhered in the structure, was measured by it, played through it, or whether the bridge simply pointed to some vision beyond itself.[4] In worksheets of the spring and summer of 1926, Crane tries out these possibilities by changing prepositions:

>   [with] [its]
> And through the cordage, notching *its white* call
>   [after]
> Arch *into* arch, from seamless tides below,
> [With]
> *Their* labyrinthine mouths of history.[5]

The "cordage notching with its call" implies some progression just as "arch *after* arch" does, but this possibility is written out in the final choice, "One arc synoptic of all tides below." Again, in this same draft, the important fourth stanza deals directly with the question of vision, and it locates the source of vision not in the bridge, as in the final version, but in dreams:

>   and *soar* [*thread*] [delve]
>   [cipher curves]
> With *curves* of sleep *into* what *lakes* what skies contain
> The mythic laugh of spears.[6]

Questions of whether to use *up* or *of* or *with* plagued Crane throughout the drafts. In some sense, the final version refused to settle definitely on one location. The vision was "*through* the bound cable strands," "*Up* the index of night," "*Onward* and *up*," but also "*In* myriad syllables," "*In* single chrysalis," and finally, "*To* wrapt inception" "*through* blinding cables." Vision seems to run *through* the bridge, *upward* from it, *toward* an "Everpresence, *beyond* time" (italics mine). Thus, the significance of the bridge is never clear; meaning inheres in it and beyond it. By seeing the bridge both as a man-made creation of wholeness and the sign by which such wholeness "beyond time" could be apprehended, Crane created a structure false to the actual fact from which this symbol was abstracted and false also to the radical energy that inspired Crane's long poem. Crane made his bridge an icon—harp, altar, pledge, myth—but no bridge. And by calling the bridge "Answerer of all," he gave his poem a resolute closure and a preordained order that his creative proclivities could never sustain.

His was not an imagination either satisfied with or longing for answers or the forms that answers would contain. In "The Broken Tower," one of the last poems he wrote, he finally acknowledged that his song was a "long-scattered score / Of broken intervals," the song made when "the bells break down their tower; / And swing I know not where." It is the radical energies which these bells represent, energies that will not be contained in towers or rigid forms, that inspired Crane's poetry from beginning to end. But in undertaking to write *The Bridge*, Crane attempted to channel these disruptive energies into an essentially conservative form and end.

The impulse to write the great myth of America came from Crane's reading of *The Waste Land*, among other sources. After Eliot's "perfection of death—nothing is possible in motion but a resurrection of some kind," Crane wrote (LHC 115). And a few months later, he elaborated this notion in a letter to Alfred Stieglitz, whose work he admired: "The city is a place of 'brokenness,' of drama; but when a certain development in this intensity is reached a new stage is created, or must be, arbitrarily, or there is a foreshortening, a loss and a premature disintegration of experience" (LHC 138).

Crane's initial aim was to locate what he calls here variously "spiritual events," "resurrection," a "new stage," in some relation to the new forms of the modern city. His ambition would always be toward the whole, a conversion of parts into wholes. Thus, the Brooklyn Bridge becomes "steeled Cognizance," "intrinsic Myth," "Deity's glittering Pledge," "whitest Flower." This willed equivalence is another manifestation of beginning at the end. But such a method is not without its hazards. In equating nature, technology, and the supernatural, Crane mended the "brokenness" of the modern city by denying the city's modernity and history. Renaming the bridge, Crane not only denied its bridgeship but left himself no space in which to write his poem.

Crane seemed to be aware of the disparity between a vision that is apprehended as complete in itself and a poem that re-

mained to be written. In "Atlantis," in the very heart of his ec-
stasy, he says,

> O Choir, translating time
> Into what multitudinous Verb the suns
> And synergy of waters ever fuse, recast
> In myriad syllables,—Psalm of Cathay!

The exact mood is hard to grasp here largely because the verb
moves in at least two directions. The "Choir" seems to be in
apposition to the Bridge, which is addressed in the line before,
and thus we may read these lines as affirming the bridge's connective quality and fusing powers: time and verb, sun and water
or sky and earth. But the phrasing unsettles that confidence:
"Into what multitudinous Verb" might be followed by a question
mark. Here it is in the form of an exclamation, but an exclamation with a question: the poet cannot imagine, can only marvel
at whatever will be produced by this fusion. The lines then go
on into the imperative: "recast / In myriad syllables." The translation and fusion appear to be reversed here, and one "multitudinous Verb" is itself to be translated into "myriad syllables."
In turn, these syllables are to be translated into the "Psalm of
Cathay." So the single and the many, the whole and the part,
fuse and refuse to adhere in these lines.

Crane was committed to the "Vision-of-the-Voyage," the
"Verb," the "Psalm," to the whole; and these lines, in their refusal to parse, testify to his desire for that wholeness in every
word, every line, every stanza, and yet such a desire had a de-
stabilizing effect on connections of words or lines into a total
structure. The poem that remained for Crane to write had to be
constructed word by word, and his real task was to negotiate
between whole and part, something that was impossible if every
part were conceived as a whole. As the poet leaves "the haven"
of the bridge in "Atlantis," he cannot relinquish this vision of
wholeness. He does not go far before he sees "still the circular,
indubitable frieze / Of heaven's meditation." Although "Eyes

stammer through the pangs of dust and steel," they see *still* the "indubitable frieze." They cannot see parts; they can see only the whole, "one song devoutly binds." Such evidence cannot compose a poem, or rather it does not lead to any indication of the poem's constituent parts. Significantly here the poet imagines that he "backward fled" to "time's end." The direction of the flight is accurate; he must go back to the beginning in order to trace the process by which "time" was translated into a "Verb." But his destination, "at time's end," is peculiar if prophetic of Crane's paradoxical backward flight to the end from this magnificent early conclusion.

The experience of the backward flight in these lines of "Atlantis" is simply an optical illusion. The poet imagines himself on a boat leaving the harbor, although he experiences it as the harbor itself moving: "harbor lanterns backward fled the keel." But the optical illusion embodies a persistent way of seeing. As he wrote various sections of the poem, Crane moved away from his ending, and his vision of the bridge as an icon faded in the process. He came to the end of time, his own time and that of his poem, by a creative withdrawal from his initiating impulse. Far from leading up to the ending, the poem was written away from it.

The route was not entirely direct, as the order of composition of the actual sections clearly indicates. Crane moved back and forth, writing in the summer of 1926 the first section and the final version of the last, then going back in time to "Cutty Sark," "Ave Maria," and "The Dance," then forward to the present in "The Tunnel," "Three Songs," and "Harbor Dawn," and then both back and forward again to start work on "The River." This order is all the more curious because Crane had already established where each section would fit into the final structure, and it would have been possible to write each in the sequence in which it was to appear. In fact, Crane himself seemed struck by the wayward progress of his work, writing to Waldo Frank, "All sections moving forward now at once! I didn't realize that a bridge is begun from the two ends at once," and later, "I skip from one section to another now like a sky-gack [*sic*] or girder-jack" (LHC 270, 272). He concluded his remarks to Frank: "The accumulation of impressions and concepts gathered the last several years and constantly repressed by immediate circumstances are having a chance to function, I believe. And nothing but this large form would hold them without the violence that mar [*sic*] so much of my previous, more casual work" (LHC 272).

Crane's statement is interesting for its curious insistence both on an organizing larger form and the free functioning of concepts. Large form, in Crane's view, would not do violence to impressions; only casual work, by which Crane seems to mean shorter work without the design of *The Bridge*, violates. He is simply describing here the freedom and expansiveness he felt in writing a long poem. But these comments also reveal a certain ambivalence toward form: it should contain an accumulation of impressions but not be casual; it should order but not violate. The parts of *The Bridge* would not have been written without a conception of the whole, and yet the whole was never fully composed of the parts.

With these conflicting views, Crane could of course justify writing the sections in any order they "popped out," as he described his creative process. He could write as he was inspired to write, and still compose parts of a preplanned poem; he could be both Whitman and Poe. But *The Bridge* was neither conceived nor written as an open-ended poem in the style of *Leaves of Grass*. From the very start, Crane knew where he was going and toward what end, and individual sections were written to be placed into a predetermined scheme. At the same time, Poe's carefully plotted poem could not serve Crane as a model, committed as he was to inspiration and to the simultaneous creation of all parts.

Crane's method of composition indicates another curious by-product of his degenerative form. He seemed to work in double sets, as if one expression inspired its opposite and peculiarly related form. After writing the last and first sections, he wrote another double set—"Ave Maria," the beginning of American history, and "The Tunnel," the end or present day. He then moved further toward the center of the poem to a set of love poems—"The Dance," a hymn to the fertile Indian princess and an invocation to historical origins, and its opposite, "Three Songs," a trilogy on the sterility of modern love. The sections thus balance each other and forestall the poem's forward movement: the despair and weak faith of "The Tunnel" correspond to the faith and fear of "Ave Maria," and the lust of "The Three Songs" responds to the passion of "The Dance." The desire to state and restate and unstate, to project one vision and then imagine an alternate and contradictory vision, indicates some of Crane's hesitancy about a developing structure, a doubt at the heart of his celebratory faith, a self-fulfilling fear of failure.

The sustained period of work on *The Bridge* in 1926 produced the poem's second section, "Ave Maria," which offered a possibility for locating the origin of Crane's subject in Columbus' voyage of discovery. Here is where the history began. However, Crane does not start at the beginning, but surprisingly neither does he start at the end, although he imagines Columbus himself imagining that he has discovered not America but "Cathay," "Indian emperies," "The Chan's great continent." In short, Crane's Columbus identifies his discovery as the end he had set out to find. Crane locates Columbus not at the actual moment of discovery or at the moment of triumphant return to Spain, but rather in mid-ocean, terrified that the weather or a mutinous crew will not allow him to return with the "word."

Thus placing Columbus, Crane eases into the central section of his poem with a tentative confidence that Columbus, like the poet, has "seen now what no perjured breath / Of clown nor sage can riddle or gainsay." But within that confidence, there is also the unmasking fear about his powers to express it. More than that, Crane places Columbus in mid-ocean and thus in time, fitting appropriately between origin and end. Columbus is most anxious there, counting time, "biding the moon / Till dawn should clear that dim frontier," noting its passage, "Some Angelus environs the cordage tree," and marveling at "all that amplitude that time explores." In mid-ocean, Columbus also juggles space; he stands between the Old World, land of his birth, his own origins, from which his visions made him an exile, and the New World, his land by discovery but from which he is also exiled by his misapprehension of it as Cathay.

If Columbus' voyage is to mark the beginning of Crane's myth of America, his location in mid-ocean announces Crane's retreat from the end, although it clearly articulates his reticence about origins. The myth of America did not begin during Columbus' return voyage to the Old World, nor did it begin in his fears that he would not complete his round trip; it was rather an idea in Columbus' mind or even before him in the hopes of a generation of navigators. These moments are given scant notice in "Ave Maria." Nor does Crane ever develop the moment when Columbus returns to Spain to announce his finding, a moment that is another potential origin for the myth of America.

Refusing a vision of the beginning, Crane places Columbus in mid-ocean, on this middle ground where he can deny the whole and recant the dream that had impelled him to search for it. He admits that the God he worships both contains and withholds the truth of man's origins and his destiny: "incognizable Word / Of Eden and the enchained sepulchre."[7] So God's purpose is and is not revealed, and at the end Columbus withdraws into that incognizance. He had opened with a petition for a safe return, but he ends with a plea for "still one shore beyond desire." And then he breaks off with fragments: "Beyond / And kingdoms," a repetition of the *Te Deum*, and an appeal to the "Hand of Fire."

Just as there is no real beginning for this great voyage of discovery and no origin of the myth of America in the poem, so right here with Columbus Crane begins to deny the end. He leaves Columbus dangling in mid-ocean yet yearning for still more because he himself cannot close the poem. Columbus' anxiety here about a safe return as well as his willingness to journey forever mark the first stages of the poet's retreat from the idea of completion that was so affirmatively set forth in "Atlantis" and "Proem." "Ave Maria" acknowledges more fully than any other section the time and space between beginning and end, but in so doing it becomes entranced with its own in-betweenness, longs to perpetuate that and not to be a connective link pointing to other destinies. Crane's Columbus does not want to round out the journey, complete the circle, affirm the whole; he longs only for more, a vision "beyond desire," "Beyond."

This section was composed with "The Tunnel," the section that leads into "Atlantis" in the finished work just as "Ave Maria" had led out of "Proem." The double set reveals Crane's refusal to develop his long poem and his engagement with obsessive repetitions of points. Despite obvious differences, the two sections share the journey motif and the concluding image, "O Thou Hand of Fire," "O Hand of Fire." The journey of the modern subway rider, like that of the great navigator, is not completed. Although he gets to the East River, the modern traveller does not seem to have arrived at any destination. For him the journey has been "cruelly to inoculate the brinking dawn / With antennae toward worlds that glow and sink," a kind of demonic version of Columbus' "one shore beyond desire." Yet, despite this despair, he, like Columbus, is "Impassioned with some song we fail to keep," "some Word that will not die." The ending of the poem contains these mutually exclusive emotions. The subway rider seems to give up, admitting,

> Here at the waters' edge the hands drop memory;
> Shadowless in that abyss they unaccounting lie.
> How far away the star has pooled the sea—
> Or shall the hands be drawn away, to die?

He has come to the eastern shore, the beginning of history and the point from which America, the subject of *The Bridge*, was launched. In this movement backward, however, he reaches an "abyss," not a point from which to start but a centripetal force preventing any beginning—time's end, in fact. The hands that "drop memory" lose the power to write, to "account" for time and to count it. But with the question mark the poem negates such an ending, and from this lowest point it moves to the final lines: "Kiss of our agony Thou gatherest / O Hand of Fire / gatherest." The prayer in the end echoes Columbus' final prayer for "one shore beyond desire," for a continuation of voyaging, of writing, of gathering, and again Crane appears to be retreating from the vision of "Atlantis" even as this poem leads into it.

One indication of this retreat is the poem's obsession with beginning, despite its ending and its own position at the present day or end of American history as Crane saw it. The first scene projects a play opening: "Someday by heart you'll learn each famous sight / And watch the curtain lift in hell's despite." From here, the speaker is launched on a series of journeys, leaving with "a subscription praise / for what time slays." He cannot decide whether to ride or walk, feeling trapped either way in some kind of restricted form ("boxed alone a second, eyes take fright"). When he does move, he comes to a dead end, fleeing the call girl who calls out, "if / you don't like my gate why did you / swing on it." He moves along, meets Poe, whom he identifies with "Death, aloft," sees he is destined for "Gravesend Manor," but keeps on going toward morning imagined as "the muffled slaughter of a day in birth."

Thus, the beginning is made into the end; dawn is identified with a world of waste, evidence of time's degenerative process. The "burnt match skating in a urinal," "Newspapers wing, revolve and wing," the "tugboat, wheezing wreaths of steam," "the oily tympanum of waters," all detail a world that is used up, run down, begrimed. Language, too, seems to be part of this general decay. The people who speak throughout this section repeat themselves, use only cliches or degraded language. Crane says:

Our tongues recant like beaten weather vanes.
This answer lives like verdigris, like hair
Beyond extinction, surcease of the bone;
And repetition freezes.

The answer at this point is not the "Answerer of all," but rather is identified with death and decay.

Recanting the affirmation of "Atlantis," Crane is forced here to acknowledge the corrosive power of time. Time does not fuse; it disintegrates. It provides no bridge from one point to another. The poem can offer now no pardon for history, no excuse even for its own composition. The poet is isolated, alone, and his language fragments: "Tossed from the coil of ticking towers. . . . Tomorrow, / And to be. . . . / Here by the River that is East." Unable to locate himself in time, even cast out from time, he loses all direction. Still, "The Tunnel" does not end with these images of dispersal, dislocation, uncertainty, but rather with the poet's desire to gather up again, gather himself, his poem, to be returned to the coil of time, his hand in the hand of God. The great despair in this section is balanced by a desperate hope in the end, and once again the poet's genius at taking things apart reveals itself. He can undo even his own despair.

Composed in the same creative spurt as "The Tunnel" was "The Dance," the only part of the long central section, "Powhatan's Daughter," to be completed in these early stages of writing in the summer of 1926. It was a remarkable feat of creation to move from the fragmented utterance of "The Tunnel" to the formal organization of "The Dance." But this narrative of composition sets off "The Dance" from the other parts of "Powhatan's Daughter" and indicates that here too Crane started at the end he hoped he would achieve.

"The Harbor Dawn" and "The River," the first and third poems in "Powhatan's Daughter," were started, but they were not completed until the next summer, when Crane also worked on "Van Winkle"; and "Indiana," the final poem in that section, was one of the last to be composed. "Powhatan's Daughter" can be read, as it is published, as a journey back in time to the Indian and in space to the Mississippi, and then forward again to the pioneers and movement once more east. But it may also be read in the order of its composition as it charts the degenerative stages in Crane's inspiration.

"The Dance" belongs to the initiatory vision evident in "Atlantis" and "Proem," still there in "Ave Maria," and fainter still in "The Tunnel." Like Columbus, Pocahontas offered Crane a marvelous opportunity from history, a real person in whom to locate his understanding of the myth of America. Crane's use of Pocahontas suggests that in his earliest inspiration he worked from historical figures, trying to make his poem close to reality. But even here, the impulse was thwarted. Crane did not take advantage of the known facts about Pocahontas the historical personage.

The real story of "The Dance" is Crane's own search for "Mythical brows we saw retiring." Typically, these mythical brows of winter king and glacier woman are retiring or fleeing backward. They are "loth" but "destined" in their flight, the speaker acknowledges, as if his acquaintance with them were intimate or rather, since he uses the first person plural, as if they were figures well known to the community. These mythic figures seem also to beckon to those they have left as "Greeting they sped us, on the arrow's oath." So the poet is encouraged in his pursuit of them. But somehow, between the retirement and the present, "lie incorrigibly what years between." As always in Crane, the time scheme here is confusing, as the speaker seems to be witness both to the past and to the present. The Indian and his nature gods have gone, "destined" by the course of history to depart, so we may assume that their departure is "incorrigible." Yet they appear to the poet "loth" to go, and he sets out to reclaim them, to rewrite their ending.

He charts his search in carefully rhymed quatrains, as if such hypnotic regularity would itself restore the Indian gods. And in fact it does, as through it he approaches the Indian dance: "its rhythm drew, / —Siphoned the black pool from the heart's hot root." He is mesmerized by Maquokeeta's tranced performance, urging him on:

> Dance, Maquokeeta! snake that lives before,
> That casts his pelt, and lives beyond! Sprout, horn!
> Spark, tooth! Medicine-man, relent, restore—
> Lie to us,—dance us back the tribal morn!

This is a pivotal stanza in "The Dance" and in the composition of *The Bridge* because it carries the burden of Crane's desperate desire to get back to the beginning which he now realizes he can never accomplish.

Up to this point in "The Dance," and in fact in *The Bridge*, the speaker has been outward-bound, on an open-ended search for something identified here as Pocahontas, for the magic that will restore not only her presence but a sense of history itself to a world which has been cut off from such knowledge. In this poem the search ends, or at least the speaker imagines its ending, as a backward dance to the tribal morn. But to get there, time itself, embodied now in the serpent figure Maquokeeta, must "relent." To get back to the beginning, the speaker must deny history, and to deny history is, the speaker blurts out, a lie. This dilemma is deepened by Crane's method of composition. Crane cannot trace to its origin the splendor of "Atlantis." It remained as resistant to discovery or analysis as Pocahontas. Thus, the narrative of the poem's composition traces the inadequacy of the poem's narrative.

Time, Crane discovers, will not relent. To identify with the Indian as the speaker does ("I, too, was liege / To rainbows currying each pulsant bone") is also to identify with his death. To separate himself from such a fate is to undercut the confidence of the end: "We danced, O Brave, we danced beyond their farms." The affirmative vision of "Atlantis" cannot hold up against time—either the history the poem relates or the history of the poem itself as the poet moves through various stages of composition.

The point at which the speaker says to Maquokeeta, "Lie to us," cannot be glossed adequately as an appeal to the sacred lie—something like Wallace Stevens' "supreme fiction"—as R. W. B. Lewis does. This is largely because Crane has been too earnestly negotiating with history and with what he calls "Cognizance," "some Word that will not die," and these references must reverberate through that phrase.[8] To equate lies with the backward dance is to acknowledge the fact of history. The tribal morn cannot be restored except through a lie, and as the poem itself proves, a lie about the very history that it invokes.[9]

But the implications of this discovery were treacherous for the poet of a visionary synthesis. If past and present can be equated, time itself made to relent, and history rewritten so that the Indian still dances beyond his fate, then the poet's invocations to images of wholeness here and throughout *The Bridge* must rely on an equally false equivalence. Between the "steeled Cognizance" and the "incognizable Word," there would thus be no difference. The "Unfractioned idiom" would exist only in fractioned idiom. Cognizance would be equivalent to incognizance, and incognizance to cognizance. If we can deny what we know and claim what we cannot know, the very act of naming is called into jeopardy. By identifying with the Indian, Crane hoped to restore the beginning, but in doing so, he cancelled out the very notion of beginning and end.

Crane might have stopped his composition here. But it is a testament to the tenacity of his longing for long form that he moved on to write the next section, "Three Songs," poems about modern women, figures who are in their minimalization of the female principle the obverse of Pocahontas and yet doomed to suffer the same fate of cancellation. In "Southern Cross," the first of the three songs, the poet's search for the Indian princess and all she embodied has dwindled into a lustful yearning for some "nameless Woman." Identity becomes the issue here as he is willing to assign her any name: "Eve! Magdalene! / or Mary, you? / Whatever call—falls vainly on the wave." In "National Winter Garden," the lust remains undifferentiated: "You pick your blonde out neatly through the smoke. / Always you wait for someone else though, always—." And in "Virginia," although the girl is called Mary, she seems to be a multifaceted girl, at once just a date, "Saturday Mary, mine!" and then a Rapunzel figure, "Mary, leaning from the high wheat tower," and finally the virgin, "Cathedral Mary." Here in this section are all the faces of women: Eve, Magdalene, Mary. But, as with all faces and names, they are one—the object of the poet's intense but fruitless longing for the capacity to possess them through naming.

Names, both as links and as points of differentiation, had concerned Crane from the beginning of his work on *The Bridge* in the creative frenzy of the first summer.[10] To name is to possess whole, Crane imagined then, but he was to discover the fragility of such aspirations. "Cutty Sark," located in the published work between two sections on pioneers that were almost the last parts written ("Indiana" and "Cape Hatteras"), takes its themes and concerns from the poems just discussed that were written during the same period. Something of the atmosphere of "National Winter Garden" is evident in the bar scene, "the / swinging summer entrances to cooler hells." And Pocahontas' spring is here in the "skilful savage sea-girls / that bloomed in the spring." But two larger issues that came to obsess Crane as he worked on the parts of *The Bridge* take over "Cutty Sark." The process of writing had led Crane from vision to verb, from large structures to small components, as he turned his concern first to names and then to time, or to time as it issues from names.

The frame of the poem is a song from the nickelodeon, "Stamboul Nights," heard in a modern bar by a drunken sailor who recalls there his own past and the American past of the clipper ships and their explorations of the Orient. Time blurs in this drunken reverie, chiefly by a free association of names.

"Stamboul Nights" recalls *"Stamboul Rose,"* who becomes not just some pickup in a port but *"Rose of Stamboul O coral Queen— / teased remnants of the skeletons of cities."* This evocation of lost cities brings up Atlantis, a reminder for the poet at least of just how far he has moved from the fabled end that he had posited at the beginning of his poem. But Atlantis is introduced with the notion that in the mind of this drunken sailor the mere passage of time "may start some white machine that sings," send him into dawn, while his companion "started walking home across the Bridge." In this moment of composition, the poet writes himself back to his original structure, now irremediably altered in his imagination.

The last part of "Cutty Sark" is a series of catalogues—first a catalogue of reasons for trade with China ("Blithe Yankee vanities, turreted sprites, winged / British repartees"), then a catalogue of locations en route ("the Line," "the Horn / to Frisco, Melbourne"), then the names of ships themselves (*"Thermopylae, Black Prince, Flying Cloud," "Rainbow, Leander," "Taeping," "Ariel"*), names with their own histories, we might note. As a way of organizing, the catalogue is inclusive without being explanatory. It is also a form that equates everything; here reasons for trading, shipping routes, ships themselves, are all given the same treatment. Thus, the differentiation that names afford is minimized. And despite the range of historical references in the names of the ships, time itself as a divisive strategy seems to be cancelled. Just as the sailor is "not much good at time any more" since that "damned white Arctic killed my time," so the appearance here in the twentieth century of the clipper-ship era seems to attest to the obliteration of time in the mind of the poet, who does not even attempt to connect this vision with the scene in the bar, but simply attaches it here to the end of the poem.

In explaining this poem to Otto Kahn, Crane acknowledged his persistent method by saying the poem "starts in the present and 'progresses backwards.'"

"Cutty Sark" is built on the plan of a *fugue*. Two "voices"—that of the world of Time, and that of the world of Eternity—are interwoven in the action. The Atlantis theme (that of Eternity) is the transmuted voice of the nickel-slot pianola, and this voice alternates with that of the derelict sailor and the description of the action. The airy regatta of phantom clipper ships seen from Brooklyn Bridge on the way home is quite effective, I think. It was a pleasure to use historical names for these lovely ghosts. Music still haunts their names long after the wind has left their sails. (LHC 307–8)

Most curious here is Crane's notion that names evoke history, or rather that the music of names outlasts their references. Names that can slip from one context to another may not serve as reliable links in any structure, and names that have a layered context may end up meaning so many things that they serve no particular connective function.

"Cutty Sark" has seldom been read as one of the strongest sections of *The Bridge*, yet it was written right after the very powerful "Ave Maria." Along with "The Dance," these poems are Crane's first efforts to deal with points in American history, to find some connection between the present and the past, to locate the origin of the "Atlantis" vision in time and space. Yet they also undercut their connections, resist their purpose, and remain suspended in a drunken haze or frenzied trance.

As Crane moved in toward the center of his long poem in that first burst of creativity, starting "The Harbor Dawn" and "The River" before he put his work aside, he moved further and further away from the power that in "Atlantis" he called "arching strands of song." The "many twain" that he was moved to embody in "single chrysalis" in that final section pulled apart as he wrote. The poet seemed conscious in mid-poem of the need to bring various strands together, and he tries to compensate for the dispersal of his poem by imagining his task as an act of weaving: in "Cutty Sark" dreams "weave the rose," or "weave / those bright designs the trade winds drive," or in "The Harbor

Dawn" the speaker urges the "blessed" one beside him to "weave us into day." Like Melville's weaver god, this figure is unseen but felt, her "signals dispersed in veils." However, her mysterious and fleeting presence mirrors the mystery of those activities—so central now to Crane—of weaving, uniting, completing.

As the last great section of *The Bridge* to be written, "The River" is the most desperate in its desire to weave the various strands of the poem together, the most far-ranging in the material it includes, but it is also the most revisionary. In the Mississippi River, Crane finds at last the image that will serve his purposes. It is not the bridge, not even *a* bridge. But as an energy and force, it is a more appropriate image for what Crane now sees he can do with the subject he has set himself. As he comes into the image very gradually and tentatively, almost as if he were afraid of it, he is possessed by a language that can serve him. But if his comments to Kahn are any indication, Crane seemed almost totally oblivious to the power of this most powerful section of *The Bridge*. He felt that he had simply approached the Indian world which, he claims, "emerges with a full orchestra in the succeeding dance" (LHC 307). In many ways, "The River" is a more elaborate and powerful version of "The Dance." Here there is no false equivalence, but a slow, gradual, and steady movement from one time to an earlier time.

The section opens with what Crane identified as jazz rhythm, always his favorite notion of how to embody speed, but this section is more significant for its obsession with names than for its rhythms. Here Crane opens with a list of trade names—labels: "Tintex—Japalac—Certain-teed Overalls ads." Yet, he concludes immediately, with all the labels we are still unable to find meaning, to read sermons in "RUNning brooks." Such names do not signify anything, especially now fifty years after the poem was written. Only the poem's hobos who are left behind by the train, which is called significantly the Twentieth-Century Limited, know names that are attached to meaning: "watermelon days," "Booneville" for early trouting. Their wisdom stems from experience, not from reading, and from a true knowledge of time. They can identify differences in time and space. For such travellers willing to abandon themselves to the continent, the midnights are "rumorous," and dreams "beyond the print that bound her name." All that has been taken in by the word will become "Dead echoes!" in comparison to the touch of "her body." As the gloss notes indicate, the land must be approached by getting away from names or renaming, "*knowing her without name*" "*nor the myths of her fathers.*" Typically, Crane undercuts his poem's purpose in his acceptance of namelessness, mythlessness, and yet he continues to name and to search for myths.

To make this contact, the "Pullman breakfasters" are urged to "lean from the window," "gaze absently below," "turn again and sniff once more—look see." In this movement toward the river, the travellers also relinquish themselves to time: "For you, too, feed the River timelessly. / And few evade full measure of their fate"; "Down, down—born pioneers in time's despite." The movement continues its downward plunge into the earth, "Damp tonnage and alluvial march of days," "O quarrying passion, undertowed sunlight!"

The Mississippi River has become here the model of signification that the bridge, as Crane conceived of it, never could be. In Crane's terms, the bridge was a completed structure, a symbol of completion and wholeness, a sign of man's ability to conceive of such a view, but in its iconicity not very useful as a model for a long poem's structure. By contrast, the river spreads, flows, lengthens, throbs, "heaps itself free," fades, "lifts itself from its long bed," moves always by "its one will—flow!" In the strong final image, the river reveals its power as arising from its progress, its length and slowness, its accession to time:

> —The Passion spreads in wide tongues, choked and slow,
> Meeting the Gulf, hosannas silently below.

These lines are puzzling. But they pay tribute to difference, to difficulty, to two forces meeting, and to silence. In short, they acknowledge meaning as something achieved through time and space. The "Passion" has tongues and presumably speaks; and, identified as it is here with the Mississippi River and with time as well as space, it suggests that only by acknowledging and not obliterating the course of time and our own implication in it can we sing. In this sense, these silent hosannas recall Columbus' *Te Deum* as a hymn of praise that is also in part a plea for continuation. Almost finished with his long poem, Crane at this point could acknowledge time and change, the time he had taken in getting to "The River" and time as an avenue to meaning. This section marks Crane's slow progression toward meaning not given at the beginning but achieved in the writing, an idea he dismissed at the beginning of his writing and resisted until it alone would provide him with some consolation.

The long poem has become the product of various stages of composition—the opening poet declaring the sufficiency of beginning and the concluding poet acknowledging the triumph of the end. But because Crane wrote the poem in a different sequence from the one which we read, the beginning sufficiency comes to the readers at the end, when it has been seriously undercut by the actual final composition. Once Crane found the image that would serve him as a structural model, the river gathering strength as it goes, he did not go on to write better than he ever had before. It must be admitted that "The River" marked the end of Crane's great productivity. He neither went back to revise sections written earlier nor was he able to project better sections still ahead. He finished "The River" in 1927 along with "Van Winkle." "Van Winkle" is not a major contribution to the long poem, although it is a fuller acknowledgment of time than Crane had achieved before.

The three remaining sections of *The Bridge* were not written until 1929, under the compulsion to finish inspired by an offer from Harry and Caresse Crosby, editors of the Black Sun Press, to publish the entire poem. These sections, "Cape Hatteras," "Quaker Hill," and "Indiana," are generally judged the weakest

in the long poem, evidence that the progress of the poem ex-
acted a toll on the poet's creative energies. The various ways in
which these poems are overwritten suggest the extent to which
Crane was straining at the end, trying desperately to pull the
whole poem together or at least to fill in the gaps. But each of
these poems reveals some knowledge of what had gone wrong.
Behind the bombast and repetition of "Cape Hatteras," means
by which Crane hoped to cover the emptiness of its subject, the
poet is remarkably candid. He says, to his predecessor, for example, "Walt, tell me, Walt Whitman, if infinity / Be still the
same as when you walked the beach." It is a despairing plea, a
desire to escape his task on the grounds of the monstrosity of
historical development, but it is also a concession to time and
the fantastic differences it could produce. At the end of "Cape
Hatteras," Crane insists on both the "Open Road" and the "rainbow's arch," the extended, extending journey and the finished
form, ambitions reminiscent of Columbus' mutually exclusive
desires to return home and to keep on voyaging.

In contrast to "Cape Hatteras" and its inflated language, "Indiana" is rigidly controlled in binding rhyme schemes, artificial
sentence structures, and sentimentalized scenes. The plea is the
mother's regressive wish to bind her son to her through need
and guilt and pity. Still, despite the wordiness of this poem, the
mother here, like the poet, has learned a healthy disrespect for
words, taken in as she has been by a "dream called Eldorado."
Coming back from the barren pioneering venture with her
newly born son, she meets an Indian squaw with her baby, and
she offers her own baby as an emblem of their common condition and "Knew that mere words could not have brought us
nearer." Disappointed, still she has gained a wisdom that stems
from love itself and not from words. Just as she holds up her
baby for the Indian to see, so she trusts her son to write to her:
"you'll keep your pledge; / I know your word!"

If "Cape Hatteras" is bombastic and "Indiana" sentimental,
then "Quaker Hill" veers between self-pity and excessive cyni-

cism. It may be, as the quotation from Isadora Duncan states, that "*no ideals have ever been fully successful on this earth,*" but the disappointment is expressed in terms that are too cynical, as Crane concludes, "This was the Promised Land, and still it is / To the persuasive suburban land agent." The view here is only of death: "High from the central cupola, they say / One's glance could cross the borders of three states; / But I have seen death's stare in slow survey." He suffers the ending, "In one last angelus lift throbbing throat— / Listen, transmuting silence with that stilly note // Of pain that Emily, that Isadora knew!"

For the poet who had started out with the assurance that "one song devoutly binds— / The vernal strophe chimes from deathless strings," this is a terrible end. The choir translating time has lost its power. The song which had been identified at the beginning of Crane's enterprise with the bridge, with arching strands, "One arc synoptic," with connections and completion, has been reduced to a "stilly note." Crane's last angelus is a pained and minimal effort, one note rather than a song that binds. Surprisingly, though, this note is echoed by "That triplenoted clause" of the "whip-poor-will," and so desperate is Crane's need that the bird's song, even in its dying fall, "unhusks the heart of fright."

From "Atlantis" to "Quaker Hill," the progress of the actual composition of *The Bridge* has charted a gradual diminishment of vision, a dispersal of energy, a dismantling of the whole structure. The vision in "Quaker Hill" belongs only to the cows: "Perspective never withers from *their* eyes" (italics mine), Crane says, as a corrective to his former hopes. The old hotel still stands on top of Quaker Hill, its broken windows "like eyes that still uphold some dream." In this landscape, "resigned factions of the dead preside." The elements that came together in "Atlantis" are all separate here. The past and the present are irreparably divided as time has turned the "old Meeting House" into the "New Avalon Hotel," "highsteppers" replace the "Friends," "Powitzky" takes over from "Adams." The poet finally admits that the "slain Iroquois" and "scalped Yankees" are not one identity but two, and he must "Shoulder the curse of sundered parentage" "With birthright by blackmail." He is left now with "the arrant page / That unfolds a new destiny to fill." The "arrant page" of the poem has wandered away from the "clear direction" promised in "Atlantis." The "orphic strings" do not "leap and converge" at this end as they promised to do at the beginning. And the poet has no time to "fulfill" his "new destiny," finished as he is with the structure he had set out years before that had completely drained his creative energies.

The Bridge as Crane wrote it and *The Bridge* as we read it are quite different structures. The first closes on a "stilly note / Of pain," the second on "One Song, one Bridge of Fire!" Crane stood by his original structure as the years went by, and as he produced within it a series of sections that threatened its stability. As published, *The Bridge* can hardly be read as a sequence, if we mean by that term a series with continuity and connection. It moves erratically through history from Columbus to the present and then back into the far past of the Indian and up again to the near past of the pioneer and the clipper ships, and forward into World War I and the subway. And even within these sections, the movement is back and forth, Walt Whitman and Edgar Allan Poe appearing in the modern world as the poet merges into the old world.

But, as planned and published, *The Bridge* seems to be designed to affirm unity and wholeness while accommodating certain historical points, or rather an interpretation of American history as itself unified and whole. In the plan, the affirmation and the proof were one. This overall structure had necessarily to be abandoned as soon as Crane began to focus on all the sections between beginning and end. If they were to be written, they had to be differentiated, separated from the wholeness and unity, and made particular. Thus differentiated, they were either not part of the whole, since no principle of unity was acknowledged, or they were only part of an overdetermined unity where one word, one time, one event, was the same as any other. The vision of "Atlantis" and "Proem" did not acknowledge time, either the time of American history or the time of the poem's composition.[11] It was the middle sections of *The Bridge*, as they negotiated with historical moments and their own creative history, that had to wedge open a space for themselves in the larger structure. In the process they threatened the unity, the equivalence of beginning and end, but they made the long poem possible. Without the original plan, the individual sections might never have been written or, if written, might have simply proliferated to no end, so that Crane's original determination did provide some stability. However, had the original idea not been held in abeyance, shifted around, bypassed, or dismantled at points, the long poem would not have been written. As this narrative of composition suggests, *The Bridge* degenerated in vision and in verbal power, but it also grew through the means of such degenerative form.

4 *Paterson*

IF HART CRANE had the ending of a poem for which he could imagine no beginning, it may be said of William Carlos Williams that he worked altogether in the other direction. Early in Williams' career, Wallace Stevens detected this tendency for beginnings and suggested that he remedy it since, he wrote to Williams, "to fidget with points of view leads always to new beginnings and incessant new beginnings lead to sterility" (SE 12). Williams contested Stevens' point in his "Prologue to *Kora in Hell*," arguing instead that his "brokenness" of composition and the "instability" of his improvisations made him "master of a certain weapon which he could possess himself of in no other way" and provided him with "that attenuated power which draws perhaps many broken things into a dance giving them thus a full being" (SE 14).

Williams' work is marked by incessant new beginnings because for him, as he claims in *The Great American Novel*, "every-thing exists from the beginning" (GAN 9), but even more than that, each beginning in his poetry begot a new beginning.[1] His faith in beginnings is established in the preface to *Paterson*, pub-lished with Book I in 1946 and thus antedating the ending of the full *Paterson* by more than a decade. This passage may be a par-odic reference to *Four Quartets*, but it does signify Williams' in-terest in beginnings. He writes:

> For the beginning is assuredly
> the end—since we know nothing, pure
> and simple, beyond
> our own complexities.
>
> (P 3)

This confident beginning would appear to offer every oppor-tunity for an extended composition. Yet, when the beginning is *assuredly* the end, the long poem will appear redundant, can-celled rather than anticipated by this opening. The determinism of the beginning is as limiting as Crane's overdetermined ending, and Williams, like Crane, found himself almost immediately at odds with it. He was to discover that the end would reveal com-plexities unknown to the beginning, but he moved into the composition of a long poem with other hopes. He wanted the long form to experiment with form, to test the fullness of being that could be created from a broken construction. The short poem had only a limited charge. Like every other writer of long poems, Williams wanted more. His problem was how to get more when he imagined he had everything from the beginning.

Nonetheless, the beginning of this long poem is not easy to locate. *Paterson* may begin in the delineaments of the giants that open *Paterson I*, or in the preface to that poem (which identifies beginning as end), or in the headnote which announces the pro-gram, or in the author's note which lays out the overall scheme of the poem. Or, it may begin in earlier published fragments of the poem or in comments Williams made on the progress of his work, or even in the manuscripts.[2] But like Chinese boxes, every beginning for *Paterson* has another beginning within it. There is no certainty about when or where Williams began writing *Paterson*, no clarity about what he had in mind at the start, no simple way to identify what developments initiated changes in his conception of the poem.

Nor can the progress of the composition be charted. Williams composed this poem over a number of years, starting perhaps as early as 1927. He published it book by book in a period of twelve years from 1946 to 1958, certainly changing his ideas as he went along. Still, he appears to have planned out the first four books in advance and to have worked on various sections of each book simultaneously. Thus, this poem is not a sequence in Pound's sense of a *periplum* or "image of successive discoveries breaking upon the consciousness of the voyager." One book does not necessarily develop into the next book in conception, in actual writing, or in published form. Even when some years later Williams added *Paterson V* to the first four books, he was quick to point out its approach to a new beginning, an effort "to take the world of Paterson into a new dimension," "keeping, I fondly hope, a unity directly continuous with the Paterson of *Pat. 1* to 4" (P v).

Despite the paradox of claiming a directly continuous unity for a work that brazenly displays its discontinuity, broken composition, and diversity, Williams' comment here suggests how important the unity of the work was to him. Willing to admit changes in himself and in the world, as he does in these comments, he was nonetheless reluctant to acknowledge changes in his thinking about *Paterson*. Adding a fifth book after a long lapse of time, he still argues that he "wanted to keep it whole, as it is to me" (P v). This is not far different from his very early assertion in the preface to *Paterson I* that the beginning was *assuredly* the end. But the beginning was not the end, and Williams' insistence on the wholeness of *Paterson* uncovers the dilemma that confronted him in imagining a form. What obstructs Williams' paradoxical identification of beginning and end is indeed the poem's length, which was not simply the result of the more or less random accumulation of isolated passages (although it was partially that), but the fulfillment of *Paterson* as a long poem, an intention there from the beginning. Not only did Williams want to write a poem; he wanted to write a *long* poem, "that magnum opus I've always wanted to do," as he told Ezra Pound in 1936 (SL 163). And in the actual composition of *Paterson*, the development from the beginning was never certain, and the end not evident at all.

Thus, the paradoxes of the poem's composition reappear. *Paterson* seems to have had a long gestation in Williams' imagination and yet at the same time to have been conceived at one stroke; it seems to have generated from a plan, many plans in fact, and yet to have remained open to information and experience that appeared to Williams over a long period of time. It was the poem Williams had always wanted to write, and yet, in a career of abundant productivity, it would not come. The beginning itself would not emerge even after Williams had been collecting materials for the poem for a long period of time.

Williams' first chore was to find a form that would contain his sense of the whole poem at the beginning, allow for the poem's development, and at the same time remain open to whatever detail or insight might come in the writing. In commenting on *Paterson* after he had finished it, Williams makes a peculiar distinction—and one which might appear to be antithetical to his own confidence in organic form—between form and content. In his mind, content is finished and form is unfinished: "I had thought about it all a long time. I knew I had what I wanted to say. I knew that I wanted to say it in *my* form. I was aware that it wasn't a finished form, yet I knew it was not formless. I had to invent my form, if form it was" (IWTWAP 74).

Here was one dilemma of the beginning. Williams had held off writing *Paterson* for decades until he knew what he wanted to say, but his claim that he had only to invent his form suggests the difficulties of an apprentice writer and not the mature writer he was. Williams had written in a variety of forms before he started work on *Paterson*, and he would have discovered in this process of experimentation that the content will find its form if the poet knows what he wants to say. Williams' unacknowledged trouble was not with the form but rather with content. He had no clear idea of what a long poem could say.

At the beginning of the writing, he made an effort to organize what he wanted to say in a formal, if fairly general, outline for the poem as a whole: "I, The Delineation of the Giants (spring); II, Sunday in the Park (summer); III, The Library (fall); IV, The River (winter); Summer imagined" (Beinecke, 185). This larger scheme was to remain in his mind even if it posed difficulties as it was transposed to the written poem. Strangely enough, Williams did not have or at least did not articulate any sense that this idea of the total structure might not prove satisfactory, nor did he reconsider the outline once he had laid it down. Like Eliot, Williams worked from a plan even when the plan was unworkable. But there remains still an unplanned gap between the content that was complete in Williams' mind from the beginning and the form he was to complete as he wrote.

Notable in this outline is the conventional nature of its organization by location and season. Even "The Delineaments of the Giants" fits into the scheme, since the giants are not people but an anthropomorphic landscape. Right at the beginning, then, Williams has reduced space and time to an image, or rather a series of images that together narrate a history of decay from spring to winter—even when summer is imagined at the end. To call such a poem *"a celebration"* or *"a gathering up"* is a willful misinterpretation both of the manifest content of the outline and of the form it projects. The outline does not lay out a celebratory poem which might allow for a gathering up of images or details, but rather it presents an interpreted history and a moralized landscape, complete at the start.

Nor does the outline clearly reveal Williams' ambitions for his poem, which were the traditional aims of the epic poet, here rendered peculiar and novel by a reduction to the image. He says, "The first idea centering upon the poem, *Paterson*, came alive early: to find an image large enough to embody the whole knowable world about me" ("Author's Note," P v). Poets have always been attracted to long poems because they offer just such an opportunity to express the whole knowable world; but few poets have attempted to channel this ambition into an image, even a large image. Williams, however, committed to such an impossible and unimaginable image, found it in the city—but not a city such as Virgil or Pope imagined. Williams was not interested in the growth of the city or of dullness' descent. Rather, in the city as an image he saw an abstract landscape.

The city's location on the river, as well as its park and falls, appealed to Williams as a "knowable world," much of it indeed already known to him. The city had not only certain spatial possibilities but temporal ones as well. He admitted that he wanted to use the city as an image to pull together his isolated observations and experiences "to gain 'profundity,'" in order to write "in a larger way than of the birds and flowers" (P vii). Here, Williams charts his progress from the pastoral to the urban poem as if he had served an apprenticeship in preparation for his great work, but the outline of the whole poem belies its mixed origins as a nature poem with a seasonal development, as a poem about a particular city, and as an imagist poem with aspirations beyond every limit of the image. If the poem were to be an embodiment of the whole knowable world, Williams had not yet worked out the correspondences he required between the body and what it would embody. In fact, the body of the world and the ideas it had to embody were at odds with each other from the start.

In the preface Williams says, "the city / the man, an identity—it can't be / otherwise—an / interpenetration, both ways." This identity dissolved space and time, made unnecessary the correspondence between a man and a city, and rendered development impossible. Yet, against these impossibilities, Williams asserts in the Author's Note to *Paterson I* that it would be

> a long poem in four parts—that a man in himself is a city, begin-
> ning, seeking, achieving and concluding his life in ways which
> the various aspects of a city may embody—if imaginatively con-
> ceived—any city, all the details of which may be made to voice his
> most intimate convictions. Part One introduces the elemental char-
> acter of the place. The Second Part comprises the modern replicas.
> Three will seek a language to make them vocal, and Four, the river
> below the falls, will be reminiscent of episodes—all that any one
> man may achieve in a lifetime. (P v)

The analogy between city and man never developed in the writing, because Williams had before him a city in which the narrative of maturation could not serve his purpose. Eventually, he converted the analogy into its most abstract form: the city as a body. Although it was not a new idea, it provided an outline with which to start in traditional terms. But he could create nothing from the beginning, and he held off working on the long projected poem, uncertain about how to proceed, as he explained to Horace Gregory:

> All this fall I have wanted to get to the "Paterson" poem again and
> as before I always find a dozen reasons for doing nothing about it. I
> see the mass of material I have collected and that is enough. I shy
> away and write something else. . . . I know it is a cowardly attitude
> of mind but I get knocked out every time I begin. Too much is
> involved. Just yesterday I learned one of the causes of my inability
> to proceed: I MUST BEGIN COMPOSING again. I thought all I had
> to do was to arrange the material but that's ridiculous. Much that I
> have collected is antique now. The old approach is outdated, and I
> shall have to work like a fiend to make myself new again. But there
> is no escape. Either I remake myself or I am done. (SL 234–35)[3]

The long gestation of the poem, then, was a hindrance and not a help in the poem's construction. Williams could not put the poem together, as he had boasted he had put together chapters of *In the American Grain*, by stringing along various accumulated quotations and incidents. Far from filling in the details of the beginning, Williams had not only to *compose* them but to reimagine the approach, revive the material, renew his sense of the whole—in short, begin again. The preparation for *Paterson* had provided material but neither form nor content for the poem, as Williams discovered reluctantly that the multiplication of details was itself not an adequate method of construction.

Although Williams argued that "the poet's business" was to write particularly, as a physician works upon a patient, upon the thing before him, in the particular to discover the universal, he had to admit that a detail, even several details, did not in themselves provide an access to the universal. Only by the poet's own composition could the image be made to embody the whole knowable world. Williams had started with the idea of leaving some particulars uncomposed. He says:

> There are to be completely worked up parts in *each* section —as completely formed as possible in each part well displayed.
> BUT—juxtaposed to them are unfinished pieces—put in without fuss—for their very immediacy of expression—as they have been written under stress, under LACK of a satisfactory form.
> —or for their need to be just there, the information.[4]

This interlacing of finished form and unfinished pieces appeared to be a way of extending the poem without extending the projected structure of the poem. It would be written from the "*lack*" of a satisfactory form as well as from the achievement of such form. The commodiousness of such composition had its advantages for a poet under stress, but it also required what Williams so far had failed to provide—some need for the information that such unfinished sections might contain. Again, the problem of form was intimately tied to the problem of content. Information, if it must be there, must be there for some purpose. Williams was always of two minds about how to achieve form. When he was working on *Paterson II*, Kenneth Burke sent him a

summary of Virgil's plan for a long poem, and Williams' immediate response was dismissive. He told Burke:

> I do not believe you think Vergil formulated any such preliminary
> plan as this before beginning composition on the *Aeneid*. He was an
> alert and intelligent citizen of his times and a gifted poet besides;
> he saw a need (he also saw words) and must have felt a tremen-
> dous pleasure of anticipation. In composing the poem he felt an
> undoubted pleasure—of various sorts: sensual, sociological, his-
> torical identification, and so forth. He may, at an outside guess, have
> indulged in a bit of logical philandering—if he found the time for it
> in a dull moment! But that he set down a primary scheme and
> followed it I can't for a moment believe. (SL 251)

Here is a Virgil made in the image of Williams himself, saved
from the philosopher's penchant for prior plans that might ruin
the pleasure of composition.

Yet only a few weeks later, Williams was describing the composition of *Paterson* in terms suspiciously reminiscent of Burke's
preplanned *Aeneid*. Williams writes:

> The whole of the four books has been roughly sketched out for
> several years. I've finished Book I. So now Book II is up. During
> January and February I worked on assembling the notes I had on
> this book and connecting them up in some sort of order. I'm no
> stenographer so that as I must do all the work myself, at odd
> moments, on what amounts to composition; I've been extremely
> busy. Yesterday I finally got the 90 odd pages of the "full" version—
> as I call it—down on paper. It's pretty loose stuff, but the thread, I
> think, is there. (SL 253)

Writing from a preliminary sketch, connecting notes, composing at odd moments, Williams describes the varied plagues of
the beginning. If the material had to be assembled in some order, if the thread had to be followed, Williams could not have
expected the particulars in themselves to reveal their purpose.
The order had to be imposed by the poet, but in the various
plans for the poem, Williams reveals his reluctance to choose

from so many beginnings, so many possible structuring devices. Because he left to the composition the discovery of its form, he had difficulty writing the poem and even greater difficulty discovering what he wanted to say.

Yet his projections for *Paterson* are important because they sketch a larger structure. In identifying the city and the man, Williams uses a term he was to use every time he talked about the early stages of *Paterson*. He wanted an image that would *embody* the whole knowable world, and as he moved into the writing of *Paterson I*, he turned to the body as a territory in which he could locate meaning. But the idea of embodiment relies on a division between inner and outer, a correspondence between meaning and form, which Williams did not develop. The discontinuities in *Paterson* are constant failures of embodiment, resistances to correspondence. Williams' ambition to write a long poem came up against his inability to acknowledge the limitation of the image, the particulars, the detail, and the result was an evasion of the particular through abstraction, a grotesque anthropomorphism in which the body is distended. The poem which claims to make a start out of particulars actually makes a start in gigantism.

"Paterson lies in the valley under the Passaic Falls," (P 6) the poem opens, and "against him, stretches the low mountain. / The Park's her head, carved above the falls" (P 8). This giant embodies the geographical peculiarities of Paterson and points to the *genius loci* which, "Eternally asleep" yet "Immortal," must be aroused. Embracing this giant is the woman "like a flower." She rises above "the secrets of those rocks," embodying both the miracle of the water, "Pearls at her ankles," and the monstrous fecundity of the earth, "hair / spangled with apple-blossoms" (P 6, 7, 8). There is no start here in particulars.

With the coupling of these giants, Williams delineates a space, summarizes a history, and literally embodies the knowable world. This marriage bears connotations of wholeness for the poet, as here the conjunction of man and woman, city and park, civilization and nature, suggests a healing union, *"by mul-tiplication a reduction to one"* (P 2). The city and the civilization that grew out of nature are returned to her embrace here in a regressive gesture that seems to cancel time. But the gigantism of this opening is determined more by Williams' effort to write a long poem from an image than by his understanding of history. Such an image would have to be enormous, and here Williams simply appropriates what is largest at hand—the proportions of the landscape. In one sense, the landscape is reduced from a valley and mountain to a human body; in an-other, the body is enlarged grotesquely. Either way, the delinea-ments are blurred rather than clear, as this contraction and ex-pansion of the image obscure the correspondences that could be developed between the man and the city.

If Williams imagined he had the whole of *Paterson* in this opening and had only to fill in the details, he had like Crane a static opening that might be repeated but could be neither de-veloped nor detailed. The embrace of the giant-city and the woman-park in love was an image that told a history at one glance, but a history false to Williams' own understanding. The giant-city had not loved the woman-park but had possessed her, destroyed and replaced her. The sentimentality of Williams' im-age here is a willful revision of history which his poem had eventually to discount.

More problematic than the version of history which the giants embody is their potential for opening a long poem. Once con-summated, the marriage of the giants is finished. It can have no development. Although Williams claims "no ideas but in things," he has no ideas here. To examine what it would mean for the giant-city to hold in his embrace the women-flowers would be to realize the inadequacy of the image for Williams' celebratory purpose. To avoid that, Williams starts in another direction— neither developing nor detailing the giants, he asks, "(What common language to unravel?)" (P 7). The question suggests a justification for the long poem. There need be no end to unravelling, and if the language to be unravelled is common, then it will be the language common to all things—for Williams, either the spoken or unspoken language of love and marriage.

Williams finds it everywhere—first in an embodied landscape:

> The flower spreads its colored petals
> > wide in the sun
> But the tongue of the bee
> > misses them
> They sink back into the loam
> > crying out
>
> . . . .
> Marriage come to have a shuddering
> > implication.
>
> (P 11)

Next he sees marriage or its absence in girls from "families that have decayed," "—the language / is divorced from their minds" (P 12). If marriage is connected with language, and divorce with lack of language, then the poem which breaks down again and again enacts its own inadequacy. The beginning begins something that cannot develop; to unravel language is to deny it. But even in this effort, Williams is balked. The language will not unravel; the giant is asleep; the people walk "incommunicado"; even the poet goes away to write.

The common language in the embrace of the giant-park has no replicas in the city. Williams turns next to an image that persists in the early drafts of the poem—the *Geographic* picture of "the 9 women / of some African chief semi-naked / astraddle a log" (P 13). In this image, Williams finds another possible language of love, not the marriage of the giants but at least a counterpoint to divorce, an addition rather than a separation. This image depends upon the denial of the beginning, but it allows for every new beginning. The women on the log are a visualization of Williams' own structure—every detail a new beginning and yet held together by the first beginning and by the continuity in this brokenness, a continuity that holds the disparate elements together as the log holds the chief's wives.

In putting together *Paterson I*, Williams, like the African chief, found a form that he could repeat. The poetic lines break down, ramble off, consistently refuse to complete themselves, but lines and images reappear with obsessive regularity. A new start in a new line is both a new beginning and a recapitulation. Prose passages are quoted, worked up, interjected, broken off. In addition, the image large enough to embody the whole knowable world contains repeated forms of smaller images in the number of characters that people the poem. They provide no narrative development, but rather appear and reappear in a characteristic stance—Sam Patch caught in his miraculous jumps, Mrs. Cummings falling, and the two girls holding a bush in full bud, themselves also in full bud. Like the gigantism of the opening, these miniatures are static. They have no developed content, only a repeated form. They also represent another answer to Williams' search for long form: repetition itself as a means of extending form.

Williams' interest in long form found a peculiar reflection in his obsession with distended forms of all kinds in *Paterson I*. The book is full of giants, monsters, dwarfs—for example, the monster with the gigantic head that made a local spectacle in Paterson during the Revolutionary War (P 10), Billy the cripple (P 26), and the deformed and mutilated verse of Hipponax (P 40). The book concludes with a commentary from John Addington Symonds' *Studies of the Greek Poets* which confirms Williams' belief that "deformed verse was suited to deformed morality" (P 40). Williams' fascination with monsters, then, was part of his fascination with the monstrous, the gigantic, the form that would both enlarge and extend his poem and perfectly represent the world it surveyed.

Paterson I supports the other books growing up from it; but as a beginning and a poem of beginnings, its strategy is to break down into new beginnings at every point of stress. While *The*

Bridge had developed by breaking down the ecstatic synthesis of its ending in a degenerative process that reflected the poet's own dwindling inspiration, *Paterson* gains its momentum from a breakdown that Williams hoped would bring him closer to the energy he wanted to celebrate. But that energy evaded him, as he explains:

> a flower within a flower whose history
> (within the mind) crouching
> among the ferny rocks, laughs at the names
> by which they think to trap it. Escapes!
>
>   (P 22)

The opening image of the giants remains unexplored in the back of Williams' mind. Like the flower within the flower, like the beginning, it will not be trapped in words, revealing itself only in silence, in "the stream / that has no language, coursing / beneath the quiet heaven of / your eyes / which has no speech" (P 24). And at the very end, *Paterson I* returns to the beginning, again to underscore its mystery: "And standing, shrouded there, in that din, / Earth, the chatterer, father of all / speech . . ." (P 39).

In later books Williams will reexamine the terror inspired by the "profound cleft," "that moist chamber" where thought "has its birth and death" (P 39). But here, in this figure of the disembodied voice, he undoes the whole effort of *Paterson I* to find an image large enough to embody the whole knowable world. Earth is "shrouded," both veiled and unavailable. The poet has not filled in the details of this image in the course of his poem, nor has he come to know the earth any better than he can know the giant.

The book closes with another abstract image of Williams' meditation on the landscape:

>   Thought clambers up,
> snail like, upon the wet rocks
> hidden from sun and sight—

hedged in by the pouring torrent—
and has its birth and death there
in that moist chamber, shut from
the world—and unknown to the world,
cloaks itself in mystery.

(P 39)

It is an interpenetration both ways between the man who thinks
and the landscape toward which he directs his thoughts, but the
interchange opens neither man nor nature to each other. Earth
is cloaked in mystery and unknowable, Williams says in a conclusion hardly as affirmative and knowledgeable as the poem's
beginning. The length of *Paterson* can be traced in a gradual
unravelling of the opening image, but an unravelling that lays
nothing bare, arrives at no point of origin. The gigantism of the
opening has been further abstracted to the "myth," "the father,"
not detailed by the poem but obscured. This first book has used
its length to experiment with an extended brokenness of composition which has revealed an insatiable energy to continue
endlessly breaking down.

Starting again in *Paterson II*, Williams locates himself in another embodied landscape, "Sunday in the Park," but again the
park contains nothing congenial to Williams' all-embracing
imagination. This book indulges neither in the gigantism of
Paterson I nor in its repetitive miniatures, but rather restricts itself to that middle scale of real life. Its mode is satire, and the
book develops by the variety of its targets—Cress, lovers from
the working classes, loiterers, the Evangelist, and Alexander
Hamilton's fiscal policies—all evidence available to the poet in
his rambles through the park.

"Sunday in the Park" is a book radically divided between the
poet's purpose as outlined in his scheme for the projected poem
and the actual details of the writing. It reveals the oddities of
Williams' method of composition, stringing together random
lines under a heading that should but does not focus them. For
example, unlike *Paterson I*, this book has an organizing prin-

ciple that should give its various details some shape. The title itself, "Sunday in the Park," delineates a time and a space and should help avoid the abstraction of the first section by anchoring the book's details to reality. Curiously, given this workable organization, Williams finally acknowledges that it does not serve his purposes. "Walking," open to all experiences that present themselves to him, he adopts a congenial Whitmanian pose. But this open reception makes him uncomfortable, and he finally admits that he must *invent* his poem. He must both discover what is there "Outside / outside myself" (P 43) and construct a way of expressing it.

The narrative of composition in this poem supersedes the narrative that the poet imagines for its characters—the Evangelist or the picnickers, for example. The poem moves forward or is stalled in response to the poet's satisfaction with his own writing. Thus, the Park "upon whose body Paterson instructs his thoughts" (P 43) is not an actual landscape, but a personified field. It may be a scene more productive for poetry than the embracing giants had been, but it is chiefly interesting to Williams because it is open and receptive to his imagination. It is a space in which he can invent a poem, and he finally realizes that "Without invention nothing is well spaced" (P 50). During the writing, the park casts up a variety of evidence for the poet, but it is not always a fertile place. Here, Williams has not only eased into the requirements of the long poem, he has also made the writing of the poem the narrative of the poem. For example, at moments the walking poet is "Blocked," but he goes on, saying, "(Make a song out of that: concretely)" (P 62).

The narrative of composition is driven by this persistence until its momentum leads the poet once again to a stark confrontation with the "terror— / terror to him such as one, a man / married feels toward his bride—" and to the converse joy when "the world spreads / for me like a flower opening" (P 75). But these sentiments from Book I are not appropriate to this new book, and soon Williams is blocked again, admitting that he has made no progress. "Caught (in mind) / beside the water he looks down, listens! / But discovers, still, no syllable in the confused / uproar" (P 81).

At this point, the poet despairs and might have been permanently blocked if the poet *in* the poem had not been driven by the poet *of* the poem, who was from the beginning committed to a four-book poem. The strategy that Williams devises here is to divide his own voice between the male poet who despairs and a female figure who urges him on, saying, "Stones invent nothing, only a man invents" (P 82). This dialogue in the poem points to a division in Williams' sense of himself as a composer of the long poem. He seems here to realize the impossibility of his early desire to release the ideas in things, to let the natural fact speak its common language. But, relentless in his writing, he will not be blocked even by this awareness. He says, "A man is under the crassest necessity / to break down the pinnacles of his moods / fearlessly," and he continues, "saying over to himself a song written / previously . inclines to believe / he sees, in the structure, something / of interest" (P 85). These conclusions come not from his experience of "Sunday in the Park," but from the experience of writing a poem about it. The structure that he sees here is the poem itself, which he will not abandon.

Still, at this point Williams had written himself out. To go on, as he was determined to do, he went back to "a song written previously," to some of the earliest material of the poem, a passage from "Paterson: Episode 17," "the Beautiful Thing" interlude which he had published in 1937.[5] This passage, which celebrates a beauty "out of no book" (P 105), forms the refrain for this book of *Paterson* which is entitled, under the poem's early outline, "The Library." *Paterson III* then emerges in this peculiar combination of earlier material and an earlier sense of the poem. It is retrospective, as Williams now goes back to old material and ideas that have been working in his mind from the beginning. First, the length of time he has spent working on the poem has prepared him to make a long poem out of what earlier had been merely an "episode." Second, the narrative of the poem's composition will have assured him that, against all difficulties, he *can* write another book. And finally, the process of writing has provided him with an interest in length itself, and it is not surprising that the relentlessly disruptive style of the first two books of *Paterson* eases here into lengthier passages and longer, more self-contained, narratives.

The change in Williams' habits of composition will be evident in his return to an earlier interest in embodiment. Instead of the epigrammatic "No ideas but in things," however, Williams opens this book with a passage he took from Santayana's *The Last Puritan*:

> Cities, for Oliver, were not a part of nature. He could hardly feel, he could hardly admit even when it was pointed out to him, that cities are a second body for the human mind, a second organism, more rational, permanent and decorative than the animal organism of flesh and bone: a work of natural yet moral art, where the soul sets up her trophies of action and instruments of pleasure. (P 94)

If, for Williams, cities were not exactly a second and more *rational* body for the human *mind*, they were a second body like the organism of flesh and bone. But Williams had been consistently disappointed in his search through the body of the city to find the energy within that body, the outer form and its inner life. All he has been able to see has been a gradual stultification of the inner by the outer. In this book, Williams comes to a revision of his hope. Energy and beauty cannot be embodied; they can only be released from the structures in which they have been trapped. To build rational cities, enter libraries, construct poems, are all misdirected efforts, Williams discovers, all designed to cover up the "Beautiful Thing" he wants to lay bare. Still, he has only the city before him, the library, the poem, toward which to direct these antagonistic energies, and he had still to write the poem, constructing it in some way that would not trap the energy which he wanted to release.

In starting *Paterson III*, Williams reveals the extent to which the narrative of composition has outstripped the poem. The poem's composition has revealed to Williams the inadequacy of his efforts at embodiment. But, committed to writing a four-part poem, the poet must go on, and here he lets himself write a shape poem, the hymn to the locust tree, which both embodies the tree in the poem and insistently asks how much such embodiment costs. Like the "flickering green" (P 39) that inspired terror at the end of *Paterson I*, the "shelving green" (P 95) of the locust arouses the fear of the elemental, a love "at / heavy cost" (P 95) or something close to terror. In carving out the shape of the tree in his poem, embodying it there under the title "The Library," Williams sets out a counterimage to the "cool of books" (P 95) he is about to explore. But he is also creating a second body, a tree in the poem which is a counterimage to the tree in the park.

The cost of loving the locust tree is appropriating it in ways not far different from appropriating it with money, methods Williams had castigated in *Paterson II*. Casually then, as if aware of his collusion as a poet with the appropriators, Williams is drawn toward the library, "For there is a wind or ghost of a wind / in all books echoing the life / there" (P 95). Later, he associates this image directly with the locust, "a scent, it may be, of locust blossoms / whose perfume is itself a wind moving / to lead the mind away" (P 96). The poet staggers here. Where will he find his subject when the locust in the poem and the library, these antagonistic places, appear to be similar spaces embodying life? What new composition will come from his use of the traditional romantic trope for the imagination, the wind?

As a poem, *Paterson III* radically revises the books that have preceded it. It takes as its subject the incongruence between inner and outer, and it marks a new stage in the long poem's composition. Williams can no longer write the poem he had in mind to write at the beginning, and instead of abandoning the project, he goes on by abandoning the beginning. As it turns out, everything does not exist at the beginning, and from this point on, Williams had to rewrite or provide a revision for his poem's beginning. This book is a book of ends. Thus, the narrative of the long poem exerts its own logic, which was hard won for the poet in old age who started his much-awaited long poem with the confidence that he knew what he wanted to say and had but to fill in the details. The idea of Book III as "The Library" was there from the start, as the "fall" after the fecundity of summer in "Sunday in the Park." But "The Library," as it was written, became no falling away from the affirmation of Book II, which had been itself no celebration of summer but rather a snarling satire.

Book III was free then to begin again in another place, and it celebrates a violent and destructive force that emerges from some inner reservoir of energy as yet untapped by the poet. So the form imposed from the start made its presence felt on the poem that was to be written, even when the writing rejected the preliminary outline. The *intention* to write a long poem made the writing easier despite the fact that the poet takes as his subject a theme antithetical to his original idea. The image large enough to embody the whole knowable world, even the idea of embodiment, is challenged here.

Since the outer world has offered the poet no images, he is forced back to his own mind: "Spent from wandering the useless / streets," he hears "a reverberation / not of the falls but of its rumor / unabated" (P 96). And in this echo of an echo, this inner chamber, he comes upon "Beautiful thing, / my dove, unable and all who are windblown, / touched by the fire / and unable, / a roar that (soundless) drowns the sense / with its reiteration" (P 96–97). The unfinished construction suggests the poet's yearning for more than his mind can attain. A movement, a sound, the "Beautiful thing" intimates a world inside, "unwilling to lie in its bed / and sleep and sleep, sleep / in its dark bed," and yet unknown except as "the roar in his mind" (P 97).

In *Paterson III* Williams' method of composition is in some sense more conventional than in his previous books. He seems more willing than in earlier books to add length to his poem by including a wider variety of prose styles—straight history about the violence done to the Indians and about the fire in Paterson, again lengthy letters, critical commentaries on style, a letter from Ezra Pound, a page-long geological survey of the artesian well at the Passaic Rolling Mill at Paterson. These entries are long and generally complete in themselves rather than being slashes of details—a reversal of Williams' usual brokenness of composition.

As it traces the history of the city's fire and flood, this book relies more heavily on narrative passages than earlier books had. But it moves away from the writing conventions of *Paterson II*, denying them outright, as the poem says: "Not by 'composition.' Embrace the / foulness" (P 103). In Williams' mind, *composition* always had connotations of a cover-up, and here his aim is to reveal. There is less "composition" or "invention" here and more quotation as Williams lets details jostle against each other in an effort to get at the life they embody. The conservation of the long poem which began to exert itself in the fully developed satire of *Paterson II* is even more forcefully present here. As the books evolved, the writing became less jagged, the individual entries more fully developed, the various forms more extended, the details more realistic.

The poet's frantic effort to release the roar within by tearing away the outside layers comes nonetheless to a characteristic moment, an encounter with a woman whose beauty haunts him, and he orders her with accelerating fury to "TAKE OFF YOUR / CLOTHES!" "and purify / yourself . . / And let me purify myself" (P 105). In this quiet moment he is arrested, overwhelmed by "the astonishing virtue of your / lost body," "—that you might / send me hurtling to the moon" (P 105). Yet this moment sends him outside again, not to the moon but to his own city: to "take a ride around, to see what the town looks like" (P 105). And outside he finds there has been no change; there "beauty is feared / more than death" (P 106). Still he longs to see the embodiment of "The riddle of a man and a woman," "A city, a marriage—that stares death / in the eye." And what he has instead is "a world of corrupt cities, / nothing else, that death stares in the eye" (P 107).

This failure of the outer city to embody the inner life, the failure of the inner life in the city, fans his desperation and fury. "They have / manoeuvred it so that to write / is a fire and not only of the blood" (P 113). To write is "to break / through the skull of custom" to release the "Beautiful thing! aflame / a defiance of authority." The fire within and without comes to full flame in another meeting with a woman, this time in the basement of a bordello: "Persephone / gone to hell" "lethargic, waiting upon me, waiting for / the fire and I / attendant upon you, shaken by your beauty / Shaken by your beauty" (P 125). This indestructible beauty arouses violence as it expresses the violence of passion, "black plush, a dark flame" (P 128). It is a "defiance of authority," leaving the author in the poem shaken and anxious to bring the mind back to the page, where he sets down "a dry beauty of the page— / beaten by whips" (P 128).

Every book of *Paterson* has its inner checks and cancelling devices, and *Paterson III* is most extreme. Exhausted by his own composition, Williams finds that "there rises / a counterpart, of reading, slowly, overwhelming / the mind" (P 130). The stream rushes the drowned dog "toward Acheron . Le Néant" (P 132), and the poet appears willing to follow, unable to lift *The Book of Lead* (P 134). In time he catches himself, urging, "somehow a man must lift himself / again— / again is the magic word . / turning the in out : / Speed against the inundation" (P 135). The flood recedes and leaves him with "—fertile (?) mud. / If it were only fertile" (P 140). Here, surrounded by "a decay, a choking / lifelessness," he despairs:

How to begin to find a shape—to begin to begin again,
turning the inside out : to find one phrase that will
lie married beside another for delight . ?
—seems beyond attainment .

                              (P 140)

He is left here with his old anxiety about beginning, about the
form that will allow him to turn out or release the energies
within him, but for the first time he seems concerned with the
need to marry phrase with phrase, in short to create a form by
union rather than by separation or breakdown. At the end of
this book, he returns to the shape of the giants and to the roar of
the falls—the language—that had echoed in his mind at the
opening of the book, and here he begins to begin again.

But the beginning again is again in two antithetical directions: "Not until I have made of it a replica / will my sins be
forgiven," he says, and yet adds, "And yet, unless I find a place //
apart from it, I am its slave, / Its sleeper, bewildered—dazzled /
by distance" (P 145). A replica or a place apart, the poem copies
or it creates. In the final image, Williams sustains both
possibilities:

                    I must
find my meaning and lay it, white,
beside the sliding water: myself—
comb out the language—or succumb.
                    (P 145)

The poet will replicate the cascade in his language, but it will be
his own meaning from the language he has untangled. Still, his
final desire is, as his first had been, "Let / me out!" (P 145). He
has still to find some means by which to turn the inside out,
release the energies within, and to embody without burying
them. What he has done so far, far from encouraging him as
an achievement, is a trap and he wants to be released from his
own text.

Instead of the familiar opening delineation of the landscape, *Paterson IV*, entitled "The Run to the Sea," opens with "An Idyl," the first extended dialogue in the poem. The two women who speak are really, like all of Williams' characters, not individuals so much as attitudes: the one, all energy and vulgarity, the other apparently all sophistication and sterility, although as time goes on she proves to be kindly and loving as well. The discontinuity of their dialogue is its most striking quality. For the poet who was looking for one phrase to lie married beside another for delight, this passage is exasperatingly disjunctive, and it does not seem entirely a coincidence that this book, with its lesbian interlude, marks the end of Williams' fascination with marriage as a model of form. The long poem, which started out as *"a gathering up," "by multiplication a reduction to one"* (P 2)—in short as a marriage poem—is just about to discover a new ordering principle.

The lecture on atomic fission that inspires the second section of *Paterson IV* was deeply embedded in Williams' personal past. It had been some twenty-five years before that he had taken his son to the lecture. It surfaces here first as a story about the poet's own life, the need he feels to inspire an interest in his son when perhaps the best thing that he could do for him would be to die, and then as a story of Mme. Curie's life. And suddenly the idea appears:

A dissonance
in the valence of Uranium
led to the discovery

Dissonance
(if you are interested)
leads to discovery.
(P 176)

With that, the poet has the metaphor he needs: "Uranium, the complex atom, breaking / down, a city in itself, that complex / atom, always breaking down" (P 178). Here is the model of form which Williams has been using throughout the poem. Marriage, unity, consonance, have led to no discovery for him. In this example, dispersal, separation, dissonance, prove to be, as they have been all along in Williams' verse, the operative principle. For Williams the city has not been a second body but always a form breaking down into disparate forms in the poet's relentless search for form. The model settles Williams' problems about how to turn the inside out; mysteriously the outside will break down, the inside will break through, manifest itself, the energy be released.

This passage and Williams' discovery that dispersal rather than marriage begets the poem recalls Hart Crane's long retreat from the unity of the bridge. As Crane wrote on, he moved away from the vision that had inspired him to start his poem. His longing in the poem always for something "beyond" articulated an uneasiness with his composition, but even more it registered his desire for an inspiration that the poem could not fulfill, for wordless ecstatic moments beyond the poem. The degenerative form of *The Bridge* expressed Crane's retreat from the inspiration of "Atlantis" that had launched the poem. By contrast, Williams composed from an accumulation of details which he attempted to fuse into a book. Although he had as much difficulty in composition as Crane had had and the narrative of his poem's composition follows Crane's descent into despair and then satire, Williams presents a different case. Frustrated with his effort to marry one word with another, Williams continued to search for a model of development in the materials he had at hand. His discovery of the atom breaking down as an analogy for his own poetic method was a stunning self-revelation, a creative insight that fired his poem. Unlike the visionary Crane, whose poem traces a terrible descent in its composition, the realist Williams drew his inspiration from the dispersal that dejected Crane.

The achievement of the end was not the finished form but the creative freedom from such finish, the earned sense that the poem had survived its trial of composition. At the end (or what he imagined would be the end) of his long poem, Williams could listen with equanimity to the voice that has sounded from time to time throughout the poem: "Haven't you forgot your virgin purpose, / the language?" (P 187). His answer in due course is "Virtue, / my kitten, is a complex reward in all / languages, achieved slowly" (P 188). And later on, "Virtue is wholly / in the effort to be virtuous . / This takes connivance, / takes convoluted forms, takes / time!" (P 189). This is not the end he had imagined at the beginning, because it acknowledges what no beginning can foresee: the "convoluted forms" of time itself. And as he goes on to meditate on time, he recalls an early image of beginning, the first wife and the need now to acknowledge time, to "hold together wives in one wife," and the still later sense that "No one mind / can do it all." Still he rouses himself at the end to say:

> —you cannot believe
> that it can begin again, again, here
> again . here
> Waken from a dream, this dream of
> the whole poem .

> (P 200)

And again, Williams speaks to himself in two voices: one urging him to begin again, and the other urging him to end or waken from the dream of the whole poem. The first echoes the original impulse to write and has spoken throughout the poem; the second appears to be new. But like the conflicting advice in *Paterson III* to write carefully, write carelessly, these voices speak in medley—to begin again at the end is to waken from the dream of wholeness, to keep the whole poem open.

"This dream of / the whole poem" had served its usefulness. It had inspired the poet to begin in the first place and kept him at new beginnings for over a decade. It was initially the dream of embodying the whole knowable world, and that dream found its first expression in the giants and their marriage. While this appeared to be a celebratory image, the dissonance that Williams eventually discovers in *Paterson IV* is right there from the start. A man like a city and a woman like a flower are an unequal match. One woman like a flower—even innumerable women, each like a flower—contains the principle of generation that will immortalize the man-city, but that is all she contains. The man-city, on the other hand, embodies not only the impulse to possess her, but all that would hinder that drive: he is the sorry inheritor of a deadening civilization, the defiler of the woman, the reader of books, the poet himself always conscious that he is failing. Such a man, such a city, suffers tremendous difficulties in approaching the woman-flower. If he has all the power, he is also prey to every force that would betray the power. And the woman becomes in his lust for her the beautiful thing, the radiant gist, embodied in increasingly remote and abstract images until the man-city, engorged in the quiddity, can pursue her only by divesting himself of himself, by breaking down. Thus, the poem that started out to embody the world, began with the body as a structural device, comes eventually to disembody itself, to identify its location not in a sleeping giant but in a complex atom breaking down.[6]

As Williams wrote the poem and the lines accumulated, he discovered that he had not a form, like a Mendelian chart with the empty spaces all filled in, but rather a constant rebeginning and new start toward the dream of wholeness. The whole that he had was a compilation of false starts. At the end of *Paterson IV* the poem, like the serpent, is choked on itself. The giant-city, asleep next to his fecundating female opposite at the beginning of the poem, must awaken from his dream, which has taken the whole poem to detail. At the end of *Paterson IV*, the poet no longer needs the dream of wholeness. He has achieved what he could by submitting to time, not by finding his meaning and laying out the language but by letting language reveal its virtue. He has discovered no secret of marriage, found no way of making phrases lie together for delight. Instead he has accumulated one line after another, one episode breaking down into another, each new detail making the whole more difficult to assemble. It was only toward the end of the process that Williams came to see that the brokenness itself had been the magic, that dissonance had led to discovery.

The long poem itself has been an extended effort to find an image that would embody the whole knowable world. Without that ambition, the search would never have taken place. The poem could have been contracted to its opening image; but the expansiveness of the original conception had forced a writing away from that image, or rather the reconception of the image not as a static picture but as an energizing atom, complex, breaking down, giving off energy.

The addition of *Paterson V* has always caused readers problems.[7] The book seems to remove the poem from its much-proclaimed fascination with the local and the real, as well as from its willingness to decenter its attentions. Metaphysical and antimetaphysical readers alike must develop elaborate antithetical arguments to accommodate this book. It has been read as a coda and meta-poem in efforts to discover why Williams tacked this incongruous book onto a completed poem. And it poses no fewer problems for a reading of the whole poem based, as this one has been, on the assumption that eventually the poet in the poem relinquished his "dream of the whole poem." *Paterson V* is the reinstatement of this dream.

In the end, despite his failures, despite what he knew, Williams longed for the celebratory poem he had originally hoped to write. He refuses in the end to waken from this dream of the whole poem, imagining it still ahead: "The dream / is in pursuit!" (P 222). With this hope, Williams can look back toward the dream he has pursued in his poem, toward beginnings lost long ago, as "—every married man carries in his head / the beloved and sacred image / of a virgin / whom he has whored" (P 234). And he can move forward to the ongoing pursuit, to the image in the head that is still a virgin to be whored. The long effort to find an image that would embody the whole knowable world, to turn the inside out, to delineate the body, has led to this image in the head, this inside story, this desire to identify virgin and whore, beginning and end. What has been asserted with assurance at the beginning returns now to comfort and assuage the poet at the end: "We know nothing and can know nothing . / but / the dance, to dance to a measure / contrapuntally, / Satyrically, the tragic foot" (P 239).

Williams wanted the whole poem and he wanted to believe that everything existed in the beginning. His long creative life and the long poem he created did not convince him otherwise, even if he had to make his poem out of fragments that denied the fullness of the beginning. Williams had waited so long to begin this long poem that he wrote it always under the stress of the end, always nostalgic for the beginning which had been, even as he started writing, long removed from him. The strength of this regressive pull in the poem's composition is nonetheless miraculously offset by an equally strong creative urge to launch out from the beginning, to write a long poem. Curiously, the long form, which has a conservative effect on any effort of experimentation, nourished in Williams a peculiarly radical impulse—to keep breaking down the form, to keep on writing beyond the beginning—even as the poem conserved more and more. *Paterson* became more conventional in its composition as it evolved, but it also responded to this unconventional will to continue.

5 *The Cantos*

IN AN UNDATED LETTER to his mother, written probably in October 1909, Pound said in answer to her praise and evidently to her suggestion that he write an epic:

> Epic to the West?? my Gawd! ! What has the west done
> to deserve it. . . .
> Whitman expressed America as Dante did medieval europe
> & america is too stupid to see it. (Of course the result is
> somewhat appaling [*sic*], but then . . .)
> Kindly consider what an epic needs for a foundation:
> 1. a beautiful tradition
> 2. a unity in the outline of that tradition. Vid. the Odyssey
> 3. a Hero, mythical or historical.
> 4. a dam [*sic*] long time for the story to loose [*sic*] its gharish
>   detail and get encrusted with a bunch of beautiful lies.
> Dante in a way escapes these necessities. In reality he dips into a

multitude of traditions & unifies them by their connection with himself.[1]

By 1927, midway between the publications of *A Draft of XVI Cantos* (1925) and *A Draft of XXX Cantos* (1930), Pound wrote to his father:

> Afraid the whole damn poem is rather obscure, especially in fragments. Have I ever given you outline of main scheme . . . or whatever it is?
>
> 1. Rather like, or unlike subject and response and counter subject in fugue.
> A. A. Live man goes down into world of Dead
> C. B. The "repeat in history"
> B. C. The "magic moment" or moment of metamorphosis, burst thru from quotidien [*sic*] into "divine or permanent world." Gods, etc. . . .
>
> Various things keep cropping up in the poem. The original world of gods; the Trojan War, Helen on the wall of Troy with the old man fed up with the whole show and suggesting she be sent back to Greece. (SL 210)

By 1938, after three more volumes of cantos had been published, Pound wrote with greater confidence in *Guide to Kulchur*, "There is no mystery about the Cantos, they are the tale of the tribe" (GK 194). And later in 1944, writing in Italian to a wartime Italian audience, he identified the still developing structure of the cantos with Dante's epic: "For forty years I have schooled myself, not to write the economic history of the U.S. or any other country, but to write an epic poem which begins 'In the Dark Forest,' crosses the Purgatory of human error, and ends in the light, 'fra i maestri di color che sanno'" (I 15).

This move in the direction of a determined structure reflects Pound's confidence in his analysis of history more fully than it explains the development of the poem he was actually writing. Pound's conception of the poem had not finally clarified itself after thirty-odd years of writing, allowing him to imagine that he was, after all, the American Dante. Rather, groping toward some sense of the poem's form here as at the beginning of his writing, and now convinced that he had a right reading of history and its necessary progress, Pound gave the half-written poem a plan that would reflect the historical development he hoped to trace. His projections of a plan did not stop here, however. To the very end, he continued to evoke analogies, define genres, promise eventual clarification of the poem's structure, in an effort to justify his life's work by endowing it with the formal structure that, paradoxically, his actual writing was constantly breaking down.

Shortly after his 1944 statement, history not only failed to validate his reading of it and provide an adequate closure for his poem; it came close to destroying the poet himself. Yet, characteristically, Pound took the collapse of his public posture and his private stability as a basis for a new beginning, a more elaborate ending of his poem. Up to his incarceration at Pisa, Pound had been writing analytically, dissecting documentary materials to get at the truth he imagined they contained, and composing cantos that reflect this process in their discontinuity, breaking down lines, pausing over translations, repeating evidence for consideration. At Pisa, the dissection gave way to affirmation, to retrospection, to a constructive survey, as the broken poet attempted to recuperate his forces and go on. Having few materials to read at Pisa, Pound gave up the analysis of documents that had formed the basis of *The Cantos* up to this point and turned to more conventional writing habits, to continuous narrative. But the analytical impulse was the stronger one in Pound, and once the threat of the death camps was removed after Pisa, he returned to his old methods with even greater energy, dissecting texts with radical fury, moving to more and more remote sources, as he searched for evidence of good government and the right use of words.

The Cantos is important as a long work because it developed the extreme possibilities of the Modernist sense of the long poem. Eliot initiated discontinuous form by putting together a long poem out of disparate parts composed at different times and with different models in mind. Reconsidering his poem in mid-composition, he tried to impose on it the extraneous motifs of the Grail legend, which came to possess his imagination, and the result is a poem that dallies with its length to the very end. By contrast, Crane and Williams started out with a positive image, a celebratory impulse, and a desire to write a long poem of synthesis or *"gathering up."* Though Crane valorized the ending and Williams the beginning, they came nonetheless to question the validity of their initial visions, to test their expressions, and to write poems that lengthen out by dismantling the unity of their first impulse.

Pound shared Eliot's willingness to write in short sections toward an end he had not yet imagined, and he began *The Cantos* with only a vague idea of how he would end it. He also agreed with Crane and Williams that the modern poet must search out a cause for celebration and the key to an interpretation of history. But he carried these tendencies to the extreme. Unlike Crane and Williams, he made dissection and analysis his method rather than a task imposed by intractable materials. More than these other poets, Pound was driven by his work on *The Cantos*, and the narrative of its composition reflects his autobiography. The long poem developed as he developed and responded directly to the changes of his condition.

It is his extreme example that proves too the extent to which discontinuous form for the Modernist poet is not aleatory, as it would become for the post-Modernists, but is based on some basic principle of continuity. Logical or grammatical connections may have been removed, leaps in associations encouraged, language compressed, voices shifted, narratives interrupted, lines broken off, but each canto and various blocks of cantos argue a plan, develop a sense that evidence is being gathered and examined toward a larger interpretation. The method is not simply a random accumulation of details, however quixotic it may seem. It has an internal system of self-references and cross-explanations. Like the anthropological references in *The Waste Land*, the unitive vision of America in *The Bridge*, and the city's space in *Paterson*, the interpretation of history as demonstrating necessary links among right government, proper management of economic resources, development of precise language and fine arts, and personal order forms a base for *The Cantos*.

The point may be stated directly and often is: "And if the prince have not order within him / He can not put order in his dominions" (*XIII* 59), "usura, sin against nature" (*XLV* 229), "But their First Classic: that the heart shd / be straight" (*CIX* 702), "It coheres all right / even if my notes do not cohere" (*CXVI* 797). But if Pound's political, economic, and ethical positions suggest his passion for a single and orderly view of history, a reverence for Cosmos, his creative genius works in a way entirely antithetical to such order, manifesting itself rather in a relentless dissecting of materials, in a constant unravelling of the evidence he finds, in a peculiar and indirect language, in a rampant search through remote sources for evidence.

Pound is a reader first, and he writes as a careful reader reads, pondering over words, examining their context, exploring their intrinsic truths, transposing them from other languages. In fact, the readerly habits that provided him with a background for *The Cantos* proved to be a serious handicap as he began to write his own long poem. He knew what had been done, what did not need to be done again, but this knowledge offered him no insight into what he would himself write. In beginning the cantos, he announced his ambition but failed to make his overall plan clear, claiming rather that the "first 11 cantos are preparation of the palette" in which to "get down all the colours or elements I want for the poem," and he nourished the hope that he could "bring them into some sort of design and architecture later" (SL 180).

Because he had no plan for his poem, the beginning had been long in gestation, as Ronald Bush has pointed out in *The Genesis of Ezra Pound's Cantos*. Pound had published three cantos in the June, July, and August 1917 issues of *Poetry*, and he worked over these, first revising and then completely redoing them, and adding thirteen more cantos before publishing in 1925 what was to be the accepted beginning of his life's work.[2] As his comments above indicate, he had various constituents but no sense of the whole, and it was these constituents he had that made the whole so impossible. His wide-ranging interests, his esoteric knowledge, his remarkable choices, his vast ability as a reader made the larger design difficult to articulate. And Pound's energy as a composer did not match his acquisitive skills. The structure he was to create remained always before him as a tantalizing possibility while he devoted his attention to collecting the fragments out of which he would build it.

But he started the long work ahead looking backward rather than forward. *Poetry Canto I* is retrospective. Neither its own audience nor its own program nor the fifty years of writing it was to launch is its focus. Rather, Pound opens his life's work by addressing Robert Browning, whose *Sordello* he imagines he will imitate.[3] Almost immediately, however, Pound sets himself against Browning, who "had one whole man," while Pound says, "I have many fragments" (Bush 54). Pound addresses Browning in a mood that Crane was also to dramatize in "Cape Hatteras": "had you quite my age, quite such a beastly and cantankerous age?" (Bush 54). And he answers himself by saying, "You had some basis, had some set belief" (Bush 54). Yet, he seems willing to follow Browning's example by finding some ancient figure to "conjure up," if only he could identify such a figure. He says:

> So you worked out new form, the meditative,
> Semi-dramatic, semi-epic story,
> And we will say: What's left for me to do?
> Whom shall I conjure up; who's my Sordello,
> My pre-Daun Chaucer, pre-Boccacio [sic],
>   As you have done pre-Dante?
> Whom shall I hang my shimmering garment on.
>   (Bush 56)

Eventually Pound dismisses Browning with "What a hodge-podge you have made there!" (Bush 57). But the question remains, "What's left for me to do?" He asks again, "How shall we start hence, how begin the progress?" (Bush 58). Curiously, concerned as he appears to be here with the work ahead, he does not actually begin at this point; instead he goes back, tracing literature from the Renaissance to Egypt, to China, ending with the half-wish, "If for a year man write to paint, and not to music" (Bush 60). Actually, the *Poetry Cantos* settle on no method of writing, neither Browning's experimentations nor writing to paint nor faithful translations, but rather they express Pound's anxious search for a new way to use his reading and translating in the poem he is about to write. Because Pound is an astute reader, his reading has left him with two mutually exclusive responses, neither of them any help to the writer.

The first reaction to his reading places Pound at odds with those among his contemporaries—Crane and Williams, for example—who felt that the New World awaited its poet. "What's left for me to do?" he asks, even more burdened than Eliot by his knowledge of the past, his reading of literature. He has not as yet settled on the accommodating relationship with the past that will allow him eventually to use historical documents in a way no poet had before imagined. Rather, here he is thinking only of imitating Browning by resurrecting some literary figure or conjuring up some ghost that will inspire him. The second response to his reading is the opposite awareness of how little of the past and of the gods he has available. As literary evidence, he has only fragments of documents in ancient languages of which some words are irretrievably lost. But more than that, as presences the gods have departed. "What have we of them. / Or much or little?" Pound asks (Bush 60). So, distanced from those "magic moments" in literature when the gods reveal themselves in the quotidian, and distanced too from their presence, Pound felt doubly deprived. Too many literary examples and too few, too many ghosts already conjured up and no access to them, these self-cancelling reactions reveal the paralysis the poet faced as he contemplated the magnitude of his ambitions.

Pound had difficulty in switching from reading to writing. As

a reader and translator, Pound is passive before the texts he en-
counters, reverential in his judgment that they deserve his attention. Yet, the reader's passivity makes writing impossible, encouraging the poet's feeling of exclusion from meaning. The
frustration resulting from this situation is expressed in the opening of *Poetry Canto I*, a passage that Pound cites some half century later when, in the foreword to his *Selected Cantos*, he quotes
it as their best introduction:

> Hang it all, there can be but one "Sordello"!
> But say I want to, say I take your whole bag of tricks,
> Let in your quirks and tweeks, and say the thing's an art-form,
> Your Sordello, and that the modern world
> Needs such a rag-bag to stuff all its thoughts in;
> Say that I dump my catch, shiny and silvery
> As fresh sardines slapping and slipping on the marginal cobbles?
> (I stand before the booth, the speech; but the truth
> Is inside this discourse—this booth is full of the marrow of
>   wisdom.)
>   (SC 1)

Although Pound vacillates here between two notions of the
creative act (stuffing in or dumping out), both ideas present the
writer as active, in opposition to the spectator described in
the closing parentheses. In that guise, adopting Browning's stance
outside the diorama booth as a narrator commenting on the
spectacle from which he is excluded, Pound assumes a curiously passive notion of the relationship between language and
the poet who forms it, an idea that might derive from his experience as a reader and a translator. The difficulty of getting the
inside out, to use the phrase that Williams echoes in *Paterson*
later on, may have started as a difficulty of precise translation, of
reviving dead languages, and this sense will continue throughout Pound's work. But the difficulty also involves Pound's problem in starting his long poem. Standing before "the booth, the
speech," he is also standing before the composition of his lifetime, concerned with how to release the truth inside discourse,

set up his own diorama booth, with how to break into words and how to put them together in a form that will release their energies.

A new question haunts *Poetry Canto II*: "What have we of them . . . ?" And the answer is made over and over again: we have "one stave, and all the rest forgotten" (Bush 60), "Arnaut's score of songs, two tunes" (Bush 61), Catullus' "crib from Sappho" (Bush 61), the songs that all begin "*si com*," "A wasted song?" (Bush 62, 63). We have, in short, only songs and indeed fragments of songs that come back from the dead to tell us anything, and from them we must come to understand the "truth" inside discourse. Yet we do not have even these documents fully. Pound admits that he has "strained my ear for -*ensa*, -*ombra*, and -*ensa*," and "cracked my wit on delicate canzoni" and managed "but rough meaning" for his pains (Bush 69–70). The example of Pedro, who resurrected the corpse of his slain beloved Ignez and crowned her "with the crown and splendor of Portugal" (Bush 65) and held his wedding ceremonial, forcing all to pay tribute, reminds Pound that he may not have the full beauty of the text that he revives, and that even the revival may be a charade. He persists nonetheless because he says, quoting Lorenzo Valla in *Poetry Canto III*, " 'Wherever the Roman speech was, there was Rome,' / Wherever the speech crept, there was mastery" (Bush 69). So Pound goes on to try to recapture the mastery by concluding *Poetry Canto III* with a translation of a Latin translation of Odysseus' descent to hell, a passage he came to revise later as the opening of *Canto I*.

The *Poetry Cantos* are the work essentially of a reader and a translator, a consciousness that echoes with the speech of others, strains to catch some word, yet ultimately fails to take control of its materials. They are reader's notes, a compilation of interesting passages, commentary on the work of others, but they appear to have no overall point and to settle on no single attitude toward the material gathered. At the end of the three cantos, the poet has neither projected a work to come nor taken a suitably definitive attitude toward the work he surveys. His quotation of Valla's praise of Roman speech suggests that he might have liked himself to be a modern Valla, whom he had credited in his essay "The Renaissance" (1914) with starting the Italian Renaissance by his preface to *Elegantiae linguae latinae*. Pound claimed that Valla's eulogy of Roman speech was "not a worship of corpses" but rather an "appreciation of the great Roman vortex, an understanding of, and an awakening to, the value of a capital, the value of centralization in matters of knowledge and art, and of the interaction and stimulus of genius foregathered" (LE 220). But Valla, like Browning, had one culture to appreciate, whereas Pound had many, and it was the diversity of his materials as well as his unwillingness to organize and control them that initially disqualified Pound as Valla's twentieth-century counterpart.

While Pound continued to work on these three cantos—making minor revisions for their publication in *Lustra* in October 1917, in *Quia Pauper Amavi* in 1919, and as excerpts in the February, March, and April 1918 numbers of *The Future*—they did not provide him with an opening to new cantos. It was not until October 1919 that he wrote *Canto IV* and the first versions of *V, VI, VIII*. In the revisions of this period, aided by T. S. Eliot's advice, Pound excised long redundant passages, removed personal pronouns, made his passages more elliptical, and thus began to objectify his poem before as well as during the time that he read the chapters of *Ulysses* which Joyce began to send him in December 1917.[4] Joyce's novel and *The Waste Land* may have encouraged Pound to resume work on *The Cantos*. At any event, eighteen months after Pound had seen *The Waste Land* manuscripts, he had more than doubled the size of his poem and had revised the beginning three cantos into a sequence that suited a new conception of his long poem.

The central cantos of this new spurt of work on *The Cantos* are those dealing with Sigismundo Malatesta, and Pound's success in handling this material was to be repeated as he went on later to project new blocks of cantos. Indeed, the idea that the Malatesta cantos might serve him as a model of how to proceed is evident in a letter to his mother in 1924, in which he says that he is "ready for another long chunk" of *The Cantos* "and trying to find some bloomin historic character who can be used as illustration of intelligent constructivity. Private life being another requisite. S. M. amply possessed of both; but other figures being often fatally deficient."[5]

Pound's originating impulse and organizing force here emerge from a single historical figure. The Malatesta cantos are a reading of various documents that detail in more or less chronological order Malatesta's declining fortunes, suggesting in the process the richness of his ambitions and attachments and the perfidy of those who betrayed him. But the four cantos devoted to Malatesta are directed neither toward an accurate portrayal of this Renaissance condottiere and patron of the arts nor toward Pound's interpretation of history; rather their energy is expended in the translation itself, in the exercise of analyzing, breaking down, and transposing one text into another. The life and works of Malatesta appear to be an important occasion for Pound to display his reading skills and to expose the complicated act of reading. Although Pound's initial attraction to Malatesta may have been intuitive, his fascination in writing about him is riveted to the source material that describes him. Malatesta provided Pound with a subject, a surface over which he could display his analytical powers, and a focus of events, but the cantos Pound wrote contain neither the briefest narrative progression nor a catalogue of virtues. Their length derives from their transcription of Pound's efforts to read the sources, to get at the truth inside discourse.

In preparation for the cantos, Pound read the sources available to him. He had written a canto on Malatesta in June or July of 1922, and then in August 1922 he wrote: "Am reading up historic background for Canto *ix*. don't know that it will in any way improve the draft of the canto as it stands; shall probably only get more bewildered; but may avoid a few historic idiocies, or impossibilities."[6] And until 1924, he continued to work on the Malatesta cantos, verifying details in the Vatican library: "also geographical verification, cross country in wake of S.M. to see how the land lay," as he says.[7] This description of his working habits reveals in little the actual creative activity of these early years. He sketched out a canto on a subject of which he had some knowledge and an intuitive understanding of its importance. Then he did research on the details and put together the final version, or rather took apart the components that he had assembled for the final version.[8] The length of the cantos comes from this process of translation and dissection of texts.

In this respect, then, Pound's habits of composition are not entirely unlike those of Crane and Williams, nor does his sense of the long poem or the series of poems differ radically from theirs. He worked from a general conception of the whole, a conviction that there existed and that he could find historical examples of "intelligent constructivity," in the same way that Crane believed in the bridge as "Answerer of all" and Williams in the unitive symbolism of marriage. But Pound differed from his fellow poets by his interests not simply in the facts or myths of history but also in the texts that revealed them. His first attraction to Malatesta may have been similar to Crane's interest in Pocahontas, but his training as a translator and a linguist made him particularly fascinated with the source materials that backed up his intuitive sympathies, documents for which Crane would have had little patience. In fact, Pound had so great an interest in these materials that most of his attention was diverted to them.

If, in the course of writing their long poems, Crane and Williams came to reconsider their notions of unity and wholeness, this process was intensified for Pound. He could not write a whole stanza, often not even a complete line, without interrupting himself, starting over. He writes as a philologist reads, not moving quickly from one word to the next connecting word, but going slowly, seeking to understand each word through analysis, dissection, different combinations, and new contexts.

This process is endless. In *Canto XX* Pound records with relish his visit to the German philologist Emil Levy, to whom he had been sent by his professor of Romance languages at the University of Pennsylvania when he wanted to know about Provençal literature. Pound reports that he asked, "'Yes, Doctor, what do they mean by *noigandres*?'" And Levy replied, "'You know for seex mon's of my life / 'Effery night when I go to bett, I say to myself: / 'Noigandres, eh *noi*gandres, / 'Now what the DEFFIL can that mean!'" (*XX* 89–90). According to Carroll Terrell's annotation, the word is known to exist in only one line of Canello's edition of Arnaut Daniel's poetry and has been variously translated in terms ranging from "walnuts" to "banishes sadness."[9] *The Cantos* repeat in the writing the process Levy describes here.

The first thirteen lines of *Canto VIII*, the first of four cantos dealing with Malatesta, demonstrate how Pound reads and how he forces his reader to read a discontinuous text. They appear to be more a series of fragmentary working notes, assembled haphazardly as they might fall on the desk of an exasperated scholar, than a finished poem:

> These fragments you have shelved (shored).
> "Slut!" "Bitch!" Truth and Calliope
> Slanging each other sous les lauriers:
> *That* Alessandro was negroid. And Malatesta
>   Sigismund:
>   *Frater tamquam*
>   *Et compater carissime: tergo*
>   . . .*hanni de*
>   . .*dicis*
>   . . .*entia*
> Equivalent to:
>   Giohanni of the Medici,
>   Florence.
> Letter received.
>   (*VIII* 28)

In *The Poetics of Indeterminacy*, Marjorie Perloff suggests that Pound's method was designed, like the collage, to release words from the determinacy of a specific reference, and perhaps the effect of this canto is that of the collage. But it seems to me that the discontinuities of this text are the result of an analytical impulse rather than of the conglomerative aim of the collage. Underneath the text of Pound's poem, there is another text to which it refers, and the discontinuity Pound's poem enjoys relies for its frame both on his attention to that text and our attention to his method. In short, the referentiality of words is pursued with relentless vigor here, not rendered indeterminant.

This canto opens with a reference to the ending of *The Waste Land* which may serve chiefly as Pound's discouraging comment on the work before him, the parenthesis added by way of consolation from Eliot's work; or it may look backward rather than forward, summing up *Canto VII* with its comments on Eliotic men of failed will who populate the modern wasteland—*they* may be the fragments "shelved," in contrast to the life's story of the more active Sigismundo Malatesta that Pound is about to launch. The line may also articulate Pound's effort to distance Eliot, to relegate *The Waste Land* to library shelves, and thus to clear a space for his own treatment of history. These comments support Perloff's claims for the indeterminacy of Pound's work, if indeterminacy is interpreted as multiple meanings, all of which are supported in the subsequent two lines.

Here Pound moves quickly to indicate a difference in decorum between Eliot's despairing attitude toward literary fragments and his own more colloquial dramatization of the battle between historical truth and epic poetry. At the same time, these lines articulate the internal battle between the poet's ambition and his muse, especially as it takes place under the laurels which will serve him, if he is successful, as a crown. More than that, because the battle here has raged over literary treatment of Malatesta since Pope Pius II misrepresented him in his *Commentaries*, Pound needs to remind himself that, others having bitched the facts, it will not be easy to get at the truths of Malatesta. But the lines pull apart by the contrary mixture of levels of language: the racy epithet for the sedate muse, the conversion of a noun into a verb and then the switch into French, elevating the text. The decorum is not established; the subject is impossible to define in these lines. Yet, the oddity of the method demands our attention.

Quite divorced from the preceding lines and without clarification, line four introduces another subject, or rather two subjects: "*That* Alessandro was negroid. And Malatesta / Sigismund." "*That* Alessandro" looks back to *Canto VII*, where Pound alludes to the near-fratricidal murder of Alessandro Medici by his cousin Lorenzo: "O Alessandro, chief and thrice warned, watcher, / Eternal watcher of things, / Of things, of men, of passions," Pound writes at the end of *Canto VII*. The fact that *that* Alessandro was negroid makes it impossible for Pound to refer to him as he had as "E biondo," but the fact appears to have no consequence here, since Pound stops the thought with a period and moves on to introduce, surname first, the subject of the next four cantos. Then there are fragments of Latin lines and finally fragments of words, concluding with the translation of the fragments: "Equivalent to / Giohanni of the Medici, / Florence."

As a construction, an introduction to this example of intelligent constructivity, these thirteen lines are perversely incoherent. They move in increasingly disintegrative stages. Explanations can be found, allusions pursued, contexts provided for these lines; but read line by line, this passage defies the eye's willingness to move in a continuous line, from left to right. Perhaps that was exactly Pound's aim. In *Guide to Kulchur* he says, "The ideogramic [*sic*] method consists in presenting one facet and then another until at some point one gets off the dead and desensitized surface of the reader's mind, onto a part that will register" (GK 51). The opening lines of the Malatesta cantos may be so designed as to defy the eye's propensity to move quickly from word to word. Or the ideogrammic method of these lines may be a strategy for getting the reader's attention, that part of the mind that will register the fact that this text is new, a new angle, establishing new requirements for the reader. It is also a new reading of old texts, designed to reveal the "truth" inside discourse, by breaking into the form. But this presentation of one facet after another is also a way of attracting attention by elongating the form. The aim is "at some point"— that is, after some repetition—to get the reader's attention.

The fact that the text becomes increasingly more discontinuous as it continues testifies to the success as well as to the playfulness of Pound's ideogrammic strategy: readers will be made aware of the discontinuity only by continuing to read, so that the discontinuity is a function of the continuity. Also, starting with the opening reference to *The Waste Land*, moving on to an overheard conversation between Truth and Calliope, the lines underscore their fragmentary, because secondary, status. They are an insistent reference to something else, to a prior text, which is itself neither fully nor continuously reformulated, and which is at the same time also concerned with its own fragmentary nature—Eliot's testimony that he has "shored" fragments or the transcription of a partially destroyed inscription. The method relies upon a continuity with other texts as the discontinuity of Pound's lines plays up their connections with other lines in other places, from which they are of course disconnected by being included in *The Cantos*.

Pound's lines that grow by disintegrating, that continue only by discontinuities, display the energies in language's inescapable referentiality. The simple line between word and reference is coiled and played out in Pound's poems, where the words are borrowed from other words in different contexts, referring to that context and back again to Pound's context, until referentiality itself appears to be endlessly repetitive with no fixed limits. And yet the lines here are not merely random accumulations of words without some tie to representation.

Pound has before him a subject, any number of documents taken from Malatesta's postbag which he will translate and from which he will attempt to suggest a life and a style. Or rather, he will force on the dead and desensitized surface of the reader's mind one facet after another of Malatesta's life. The interplay between Pound's text and Malatesta's letters serves to remind the reader that this is only a reading of a reading, that it has all been written before and simultaneously that we have only Pound's fragments from which to construct a new reading, just as Pound has only a torn inscription to read. As an aid to reading, Pound provides in the opening lines several models for the relationship between one text and another, one person and another, one incident and another: the slanging of one by the other, for example, the murder of one by the other, the translation from one language to another, the stealing of lines, the respectful address of one by the other, the obsequiousness in the respect, the affection formalized into words and thus rendered false by being detached from its object. These are the strategies that Pound himself will use as he generates his own long poem from his rumination over the texts before him.

Beginning *Canto VII* with a reference to another beginning and another ending, Pound draws our attention immediately to the extended beginning of his text and to the continuity of reading and writing, the impossibility of beginning or finding a beginning. The conventional start in the middle serves Pound's new purposes here by attracting our attention immediately, disappointing our expectations of a story or a scene, and still forcing us to register one phrase after another until our unshakable faith in continuity as a source of meaning wobbles, and Pound catches it up again with the announcement "Letter received." Then we read backwards from the torn inscription to the address, to the writer's name, and back to some oddments about truth and Calliope and to the fragments which now seem to have nothing to do with Eliot's poem. So the poem forces a reading both backwards and forwards, again lengthening itself by encouraging a rereading. The poem defies conventional notions of the progression of the written word, even of poetry, releases the text from its placement on the page, and provides a new angle on the words, a revelation of the different meanings they might contain.

Readers who have come to these lines from different angles of vision have seen different arrangements and purposes, and to a certain extent the discontinuity of Pound's text encourages the continuers to fill in the gaps, to add what Pound has been at such pains to remove. For example, Michael Bernstein, in his study of the modern verse epic, compares Pound's ideogrammic treatment of history in these cantos with the inductive procedures of Agassiz and Froebenius. Bernstein suggests that such a method allows the poet to present single details that will by being combined "*naturally*" suggest a particular argument or interpretation. He says, "The poet, in other words, does not invent anything (*vide* Milman Parry); like any epic bard he merely arranges what is already there, apparently letting the tribe's own history narrate itself for the edification (judgment) of its hearers, the truth of the narration guaranteed by the poet's strategic refusal to assume the role of sole, originating source of articulation." [10] For Bernstein, the Malatesta cantos are a number of vividly selected episodes from contemporary records of various Italian principalities and ruling families which allow to emerge a picture of an era splendid for its patronage of the arts but limited by savage warfare, individual excesses, ruthless competition, and a profound political instability.

In another reading of the Malatesta cantos, Michael Harper argues that "the Malatesta sequence is a critical *reading* of some of the chief primary sources for any understanding of Sigismundo; Pound does not just present his results, he invites us to repeat the process by which he arrived at them: to study and weigh the styles—and hence, Pound believed, the essences, *les hommes mêmes*—of Malatesta and his chief accuser." [11] In this vein, although also discussing another set of cantos, Hugh Kenner argues that the cantos "conserve the vigor of actual documents, to convey a *senso morale* and a purpose," although even he admits that "they convey less well what the *senso morale* is engaged on." [12] In contrast, Joseph Riddel calls the cantos "a signifying machine, a machine producing signs out of an encounter of signs." [13] Behind every reading is a reader with particular skills, looking at the poem from a new angle, as Pound said, "the newness of the angle being relative," and Pound's aim "being revelation, a just revelation irrespective of newness or oldness." But a revelation of what, we may ask? For Kenner, it is a *senso morale*; for Harper, the style as the essence of the man; for Bernstein, the picture of an age; for Riddel, a sign out of signs. These readings all rely in one way or another on the text as adding up to something, coming together into some form.

However, Pound's own discontinuous method here does not add up but rather breaks down or, paradoxically, it is in the breakups that it develops. For example, in the letter that Pound translates, he himself expresses a certain concern for the clarity of his translation which is matched by Malatesta's concern with his own message, as it will be conveyed by his patron to the painter for whom he, Malatesta, serves as a patron. To insure against misunderstanding, Pound interrupts his text to translate some phrases and then to give them in the original, as if he wanted to clarify his translation or leave it open for emendation. In the same way, Malatesta is concerned to establish the reliability of his word, interrupting his message by insisting that "I want it to be quite clear," while simultaneously casting doubt on his patron's word: "let me have a clear answer." The subject here is money, and the parallel between money and words as having different values to people of different stations while remaining the same coin is a reminder of Pound's own act of translation, of the passing of one text into another. The concern with the language itself, with what it contains or can be made to contain, is simultaneously an impediment to the progress of the text, the major point of the text, and a significant means of adding length to it.

Pound's presence in the text as a reader of other readings is not detached in its reserve and judgment. Sometimes he enters the text as the avenging critic of what he reads—for example, in his description of Andreas Benzi's indictment against Malatesta as Benzi "Got up to spout out the bunkum / That that monstrous swollen, swelling s.o.b. / Papa Pio Secundo / Aeneas Silvius Piccolomini / da Siena / Had told him to spout, in their best bear's-greased latinity" (*X* 44). Pound might be said to imitate the tyranny of the Pope himself here, a reminder that every reader reads as he will.

We cannot conclude from this that the cantos are simply wordplay, Riddel's signifying machine. If Pound would school us to read historical documents carefully and warily and also perversely and judgmentally, he would not advise us not to read at all or to read texts without some regard for what they are saying. A good reader of the Pope's *Commentaries* will be able to discern that His Holiness is a poor reader of events and thus be instructed by the Pope's mistakes. But of course a good reader will be good precisely because he will always be aware of his own ignorance and of the unreliability of the texts he must read, and thus suspicious of the entire enterprise.

The act of reading which Pound may have hoped would be inspirational and integrative was, as we have seen, in his own practice analytical and disintegrative. Pound was always taking apart the material before him almost word for word. Despite the adhesive *Ands* with which any number of lines in the Malatesta cantos open, the lines are marked by asides, parenthetical remarks, by inserted documents, by words translated and then given in the original, by repetitions. Words are not always read analytically. They may be used to obstruct referentiality, to cover up whatever meaning they might be said to contain, to forestall analysis. For example, what new energies are restrained rather than released by calling Sigismundo "Sidg" or the Pope "Fatty," or by referring to any number of minor historical figures by their real or familiar names? This habit suggests Pound's intimacy with his materials, but it shuts out the reader's possibility of sharing such company. Again, the discontinuities in the chronicle of Malatesta's fortunes are multiplied by Pound's habits of composition, his concern with particular words, details, names, as entities in themselves, without connections to what precedes them or what follows.

Yet, despite its dilatory way with words, the Malatesta sequence moves toward an end, imagined characteristically both as the end and the refusal of an end—"the gloom, the gold gathers the light against it," and a recognition, rare in Pound's early work, that he must indeed end his canto. He turns for an ending of this series of cantos, with their reading of Renaissance documents, to a final document: a contract that Malatesta made with his steward, Henry, that Henry would stand "any reasonable joke that I play on you" and "joke back / provided you don't get too ornry" for the consideration of "a green cloak with silver brocade" (*XI* 52). This too, Pound writes, they put "all down in writing."

The solemnity of the contract overlays the hilarity of its purpose and reveals the Renaissance playfulness with witnessed documents: *"Actum in Castro Sigismundo, presente Roberto de Valturibus / . .sponte et ex certa scienta . . . to Enricho de Aquabello."* Treaties made and broken, treacheries perpetrated and undertaken by both Malatesta and his adversaries, were the life of the Renaissance soldier of fortune. To sign a contract allowing jokes from and toward his steward was in fact no greater joke than the serious alliances Malatesta had made and broken in his lifetime. Nor, should we assume, is Pound's own act of putting it all down in writing without its own playfulness. His reader may not be rewarded with even so much as "a green cloak with silver brocade" for the engagement, but the reader should be alerted by this ending (if the process of reading up to it has not provided a clue) that the reading contract with Pound was for the fun of it. Pound's readers have returned the joke often, sporting with the poet's own seriousness and pondering over his sports, but it was Pound who established the rules. Putting it all down in writing is a sober enterprise, Pound seems to agree, but it need not destroy the joke, and in fact it can enhance the fun, insist upon the impossible "reasonableness" of words, and insure that the exchange between writer and reader be not too "ornry."

By ending with the document on the joke contract, Pound registers as a conclusion Malatesta's zest for life, his playfulness and good humor, his generous and free spirit. But he tells also how much he admires and shares these attributes. The cantos' dalliance, breathless speed, jests, light-handed way with words, solemnity in translation, all imitate as they reflect the life that they detail. By this discontinuous method, Pound has revealed the energies of the man that have been stifled by the chronicle, and at the same time he has revived the energies latent in words themselves. It has been both a serious reading of a character often misread and a play on reading itself as an enterprise that must not take itself totally seriously. Words are jokes as well as riddles, and poems, like jokes, ought to be fun to take apart, to put together, to look at and listen to. The narrative of Malatesta is the narrative of Pound's composition.

Like Malatesta's Tempio, Pound's cantos about Malatesta are unfinished. Yet they are an aggregate of details, constructed out of many parts and out of a figure broken down into parts. These lines are not fragments shored against ruins but fragments reduced to smaller fragments, reused in another form, taken apart again, and recomposed. The pleasure is in the act of examination and not in the symmetry of the argument or in the consolation of order restored to ruins. Maintaining the discontinuity of his long poem, Pound continues to draw his readers' attention to the pleasure of words, one by one, rather than to their combination in an unbroken whole.

Read as a sequence, the Malatesta cantos reveal the disintegrative process that is evident in individual lines or cantos. The ideogrammic method of presenting one facet and then another, cumulative as it may seem, encourages also a foreshortening of detail, a disruption of narrative continuity, a presentation of one episode from which certain judgments may be deduced, followed by a presentation of a different episode leading to contradictory judgments. For example, the various documents translated in *Canto VIII* provide evidence of Malatesta's integrity, decency, literary accomplishment, patronage of the arts, betrayal by enemies. Once this portrait is established, Pound goes on in *Canto IX* to undo its positive assessment by detailing Malatesta's treachery in matters of alliances, his rape, his philandering, as well as his paternal affection, his devotion to the building of the Tempio. *Canto X*, taking another turn, presents the Pope's indictment against Malatesta, which Pound calls "bunkum" and the Pope deems "*Orationem / Elegantissimam*," and which the reader by now, with such evidence as he has, must judge as not quite either one. Finally, *Canto XI* depicts a beaten man, weakened by his own excesses and obstinancy as well as by the villainy of his enemies, yet still anxious to "give that peasant a decent price for his horses," to provide for the Tempio, still conversing with his friends " 'of ancient times and our own, in short the usual subjects / Of conversation between intelligent men.'"

Despite the chronological organization of these cantos, the portrait of Malatesta resembles a vorticist portrait—slashes of detail within a jagged overall outline. The whole life does not build up, but fragments. The general outlines of Malatesta's biography are there in the first canto; the succeeding cantos simply add more details, develop in the interstices of the full history, analyze the data. They trace the narrative of their composition more clearly than the narrative of Malatesta's life, reflecting the way in which Pound came into his insights rather than the progression of historical events.

In the same way that the Malatesta cantos multiply by dividing the record, breaking down one interpretation by suggesting its inadequacy, presenting one ideogram after another, so the whole first volume of cantos, *A Draft of XVI Cantos*, comes together. Hugh Kenner sees in this grouping a sketch of Pound's mental fortunes and a compendium of his interests and styles which he groups into a sequence with five sections: Overture, I–III; Phantastikon Group, IV–VII; Malatesta Group, VIII–XI; Moral exempla, XII–XIII; Hell Group, XIV–XVI. And he cites two structural models: either Malatesta's postbag, a clutch of documents proper to one time, or Malatesta's Tempio, a concentration of pieties and traditions, the parts finely crafted but the structure unfinished.[14]

As these cantos come together in one volume, however, they build toward no clear indication of the poem of some length which they are to begin. As an enlarged ideogram, they present facet upon facet, topics introduced and superseded by new topics, but again the juxtapositions—for example, of Baldy Bacon, the honest sailor, and Kung—suggest no new interpretation of history. Ruin and destruction triumph in these cantos, as Kenner reminds us in identifying them as postwar poetry, expressions more of their own time than of the history they recollect. But more than that, this collection of cantos establishes the method of fragmentation which Pound will use to write future cantos.

This first collection of cantos gathers together moments of prophecy, of vision, of moral lessons, all potentially full in themselves, yet seldom finding expression in the action of the canto or surrounding cantos, giving way instead to a proliferation of antagonistic activity. For example, Kung's advice that " 'Without character you will / be unable to play on that instrument / Or to execute the music fit for the Odes'" (*XIII* 60) is followed immediately in *Canto XIV* by a depiction of the politicians of World War I as "betrayers of language." Or the suggestion of the "Choros nympharum" of *Canto IV* is followed not by evidence of such music but by a recounting of various cannibalistic love stories. In *Canto III*, the protagonist "sat on the

Dogana's steps," poor and dejected, but the poem cuts into that mood with the immediate suggestion that "Gods float in the azure air" (*III* 11). Sometimes the vision is there at the start as in *Canto VII*, which opens with Homer's "Ear, ear for the sea-surge," "Scene for the battle only, but still scene / Pennons and standards y cavals, armatz / Not mere succession of strokes, / sightless narration"; but the canto witnesses this scene's fading into "Words like the locust-shells, moved by no inner being" (*VII* 24, 26). In the larger sweep of the first collection of cantos, one canto presents a commentary which the next interrupts until the final and complete breakdown of the concluding Hell cantos, XIV–XVI. These end characteristically by promising a new beginning, "That it was going to begin in a week" (*XVI* 75).

If the first volume of cantos revealed no clear indication of the poem ahead, Pound nonetheless continued to write and publish cantos. Bernstein suggests that as Pound wrote he developed two models for structuring his work including history: the inductive/ideogrammic method and the method of Chinese historiography. The first allowed Pound to represent a culture by selected "luminous details" from its history; the second provided Pound with a theory of history as exempla, the narrative of good or bad rulers who would determine the nature of the state.[15] These structural models gave Pound the means of examining history and unfolding historical details from a few primary assumptions about its workings. It is important to note that these models developed as Pound's interests changed, so that the narrative of the poem reflects the development of his intellectual life.

In the profuse outpourings of cantos between 1930 and 1940, Pound moved from historical persons to history itself and the single key to its development. In these years, his interest proliferated and his range of subjects broadened, but paradoxically Pound's attitude toward his material stiffened. In the lengthy usurious center of *The Cantos*, Pound's text becomes more fragmented, multidirectional, self-reflexive, even as his historical

judgment becomes more singular. In *Canto XLVI*, he comments
on his historical method:

> 19 years on this case/first case. I have set down part of
> The Evidence. Part/commune sepulchrum
> Aurum est commune sepulchrum. Usura, commune sepulchrum.
> helandros kai heleptolis kai helarxe.
> Hic Geryon est. Hic hyperusura.
>
> (*XLVI* 234–35)

The judgment is clearly stated: usury is death. As an historian,
Pound is inflexible and dogmatic; as a poet, he is playful, flexing
language, reveling in lexicographical flourishes. Presenting
himself as the scientist weary from his long task, Pound actually
demonstrates only the skills of the punster. The case method as
he practices it here is neither an enterprise of inductive reason-
ing nor an effort at scientific classification, but a demonstration
of multilingual wordplays.

But Pound's admission here that he has spent nineteen years
on part of the evidence of the first case details the narrative of
the poem's composition. It suggests something about the gener-
osity of Pound's vision, the devotion to his task, the length of the
argument. But it also reveals his unwillingness to sort out the
evidence, to conduct his research efficiently, to trim his task to
the time available. Even in a long creative career, nineteen years
spent on part of the first case leaves few years for the rest of the
first case.

But if the right reading of the historical record takes a long
time and a subtle reader, then the length of *The Cantos* may be
justified. In the long central section of *The Cantos*, Pound maintains a permanently destabilized text, one that wobbles around
the unwobbling pivot of the poet whose interest in two mutually exclusive structural principles—"the repeat in history" and
the "magic moment" of metamorphosis—provides a rationale
for an endless poem. Nineteen years spent on part of the evidence for the first case suggests that the project would have no

end or that the researcher is tediously slow or that the case, like the Tempio, is conceived on such a grandiose scale that it can never be completed (or all three of these). Writing the cantos in these years of his life, Pound saw neither the completion of his work nor the need to restructure the beginning toward a more suitable end. He was conscious simply of how long he had worked, how little he had done, how much remained. So he went on, collating material or fragmenting the record, moving from one unfinished case to another, with little thought expressed in the poem at least of what lay ahead.

THE END came long before Pound was prepared for it, cancelling temporarily his work on the case against usury, destroying his hopes for a Fascist millennium, silencing the poet who would address the polis, and locking him into the deafening solitude at Pisa. There he was forced to start over again on different terms. Up to this point, his immense curiosity had been directed outward, to the records he read, the civic matters he studied, the literature he translated. He looked at texts, took them apart, examined their parts, spliced them together to make a different composition, aiming always toward a new combination of many fragments. Even when the fragments themselves refused to come together in a completed structure, Pound was able to relish his unfinished masterwork because he felt its principles were fixed and sound, its plan elaborate. With his incarceration at Pisa, the fragments remained in his head—or at least some of the most memorable fragments did—but the organizing principle had crumbled. He had to sort through the pile not only to see what was salvageable, but to see on what basis he could start the rebuilding. He had always written from the inner conviction that he was right; now he found himself under the necessity of reestablishing that assurance. Once again, the narrative of the composition and the narrative of the poem coalesce.

At Pisa, he worked for the first time with the consciousness of the end—and it was this consciousness that gave his poetry the

urgency that it had lacked earlier. More than the end of the
cantos, he was thinking now of his own end, and that awareness,
missing from his more magisterial earlier poetry, added its poi-
gnancy to the writing. The organizing principle of the Pisan sequence may be, as Wendy Stallard Flory has argued, the poet's
movement toward self-confrontation and knowledge, but it is a
movement that is framed by the knowledge of last things, by
necessity, and by age.[16] The self which the poet confronts is, he
says, "a man on whom the sun has gone down," contemplating
what is "now in the mind indestructible." The mood is retrospective, but now anxiously so, the poet looking from the van-
tage point of age back to his earlier self and looking too at the
self he has become. Poetry that confronts the self at the beginning of life—the young poet or the young person setting out—is
familiar. But here Pound is no outsetting bard in the Whitman
tradition. He has already seen the end.

The *Pisan Cantos* open with a view of the end that makes all
beginnings pointless, as Pound tries to summon up words to
write, to start again. With a backward glance, he says:

The enormous tragedy of the dream in the peasant's bent shoulders
    Manes! Manes was tanned and stuffed,
    Thus Ben and la Clara *a Milano*
            by the heels at Milano
That maggots shd/ eat the dead bullock
DIGONOS, Δίγονος, but the twice crucified
            where in history will you find it?
yet say this to the Possum: a bang, not a whimper,
            with a bang not with a whimper,
To build the city of Dioce whose terraces are the colour of stars.
                                    (*LXXIV* 425)

No end so final as this one, we might conclude. For Pound,
the end of Mussolini, of Ben and la Clara, the "enormous tragedy in the peasant's bent shoulders," was beyond imagining—
"where in history will you find it?" he asks. He judges his own
age with customary severity here, but it is severity edged now

with melodrama. The disparity between the dream Pound has projected "in the peasant's bent shoulders" and the actual burden those shoulders could and did in fact bear forces a reevaluation of Pound's assessment of the tragedy's enormity.

Even his language calls attention to itself. In the bang of the twice-crucified, the mixed metaphor articulates Pound's confusion as well as his incredulity. "Where in history will you find it?" he asks. We might imagine that any schoolboy could provide ample answers to that question, as every age casts up its evidence of the end of dictators. But Pound, the master reader of history, seems to reveal a surprising ignorance of that "school book of princes." And yet of course, Pound is not so much ignorant and innocent as weary. Speaking from what must have seemed to him as a position beyond the grave, Pound expresses this weariness by the use of unfinished constructions: "The enormous tragedy of the dream," "Thus Ben and la Clara," "To build the city of Dioce." Each line hangs suspended at the beginning of the *Pisan Cantos*. But, we must ask, this incomplete phrasing in a passage about the end—where in poetry will you find it? Pound is engaging in his usual doubled discourse, saying one thing and leaving another meaning available in the margins. Describing the death of Mussolini and of his own political hope and historical vision, accepting apparently the finality of the end, Pound is at the same time leaving everything open rhetorically. It is not weariness but some prolonged hope that may account for the construction, an unwillingness to foresee and foretell the end, even as he takes the end to be his ostensible subject.

The construction of these lines is peculiar. They do not form a single sentence, punctuated as they are by odd commas, exclamation points, slashes, and question marks, but they do end with a period and cluster around the single idea of death. Thus they are more coherent than Pound's usual poetic unit. They are also bound together by their incompletion, one slash of a phrase and then another slash. So the first structuring device (the idea of death) and the second (the open form) work to hold the disparate lines together in suspension. But they also undercut each other—the closure of death, the open form.

The possibility of closure here is greater than in other parts of *The Cantos* because the surface of the text is more continuous. Difficult as it seems and discontinuous as it may sound, still this passage focuses on a single subject, the death of Mussolini and of the political hopes he inspired in the poet. There are, in Pound's usual manner, wide-ranging allusions, but even they are easier to round back into the text than is usual in Pound's cantos. For example, "Manes! Manes," presumably a repeated word, is actually two different references—*Manes*, the Latin for "spirits of the dead," and Manes, the name of the Persian sage who was crucified for his beliefs. Also *Manes* may be a form of the Latin verb "to remain." Even the references are less esoteric here, although we must know that T. S. Eliot's nickname was Possum, and we must remember lines from his poetry. The practiced student of Pound might even be tempted to complete some of the incomplete sentences, assuming that "To build the city of Dioce" might be Pound's way of expressing a fervent desire.

Still, this is no clear way to end, and indeed the ending is not clearly in view however close the death cells have brought it. The principle of fragmentation that had operated on the surface of the cantos up to this point has not been abandoned; it has simply moved to another level. The surface is more continuous here in this opening because the vision is less clear, or rather because the eyes that behold that vision have clouded. Pound has anticipated such a judgment by writing, "The suave eyes, quiet, not scornful." The synaesthesia of this line expresses the uncertainty, a mood enhanced by the adjectives on either side of it, which pull in opposite directions—toward acceptance ("suave eyes") and toward rejection ("scornful"). Suave eyes, quiet like the "suave air" later on that may give way to scirocco, are eyes with the vision in abeyance. They may remain quiet, curiously either blind to vision or blinded by it, in the same way that Eliot's persona is imagined "Looking into the heart of light, the silence" in *The Waste Land*. Or they may change, but it is not likely that they will again turn scornful, since Pound is quick to warn, "What you depart from is not the way." Pound has lost the way, and he is waiting now quietly for new guideposts to point the way to the end.

His lifelong habit of critical reading, which in an earlier time would have been his first recourse at such a crisis, fails him at this point. He had no books to read—only the Confucius which he had taken when he was captured, the Bible which he was given at the Detention Training Center, and *The Pocket Book of Verse* he had found on an outhouse seat there. Although he longingly claims that "with one day's reading a man may have the key in his hands," he knows that a lifetime of reading has brought him to his present condition, provided him with no key, and he knows too that one more day would not reverse the process. Much as he would have been tempted by the reading, reading had always been for him an analytical act. He had read to take apart, to reduce to fragments, to dissect the record, because he read from the conviction that discourse would sustain that kind of analysis, reveal in that way "the marrow of wisdom" as he said in the early *Poetry Canto*. Even when the record gave way, revealing only the reading of a reading of a reading, even then Pound kept on, acknowledging himself as a part of a process, between the beginning he could not find and the end he failed to see. For example, the translation of *Canto I* itself is layered with several acts of reading—first Pound translates not from the Greek but from Divus' Latin translation of *The Odyssey*, and he translates this Latin into the alliterative verse of Middle English, not modern English, and of course *The Odyssey* is itself a record of accumulating stories told by many voices. Thus, Pound's reading is a composite of many readings. So there can be identified no first or last reading, no final authoritative version—every reading is a fragmenting of the text. At Pisa, the books had been taken away, the "suave eyes, quiet," but even more important the analytic and fragmenting impulses were suppressed by the greater need to affirm, to integrate, to gather, and to be sustained.

Not reading now, Pound is remembering, engaged in a kind of retrospective rereading without the texts. He is adding up, not dividing now, trying to get the whole and to provide some summary. But there is no organizing principle on which to base the summary, and so he tries simply to locate himself where he is. He begins by calling out to Odysseus, trying to identify himself with Odysseus, even when he knows that their fates have been different. He goes about this task by repeating the name that Odysseus took when he was with the Cyclops—noman. Pound says, as if by way of incanting his name and thus his beginning and end:

> 'I am noman, my name is noman'
> But Wanjina is, shall we say, Ouan Jin
> or the man with an education
> and whose mouth was removed by his father
> > because he made too many *things*.
> > (*LXXIV* 426–27)

Pound uses the methods with which he has been long familiar, playing on sounds by splicing the name of Odysseus to the name Wanjina, the Australian god who created the world by naming objects. Because Wanjina created too many objects, his father removed his mouth. And then Wanjina sounds like Ouan Jin, a Chinese man of letters. It is simply a trick of transliteration, and it provides no summarizing view of the world. In this first of the *Pisan Cantos*, Pound's method seems to be incremental, as it is in this passage. It is as if, with the end possibly at hand and no clear way ahead, he might survive only if he keeps adding to the writing.

In this canto which seems to have such difficulty providing an end for itself as well as for twenty-five years of work on the cantos that it crowns, the shadow of death predominates. Pound insists repeatedly that he is "a man on whom the sun has gone down." He even says that the "nymph of the Hagoromo came to me," casting the feather mantle over the spirit of the dead as in the Noh plays that had interested Pound early in his career. Still, he resists the end, claiming, "first must destroy himself ere others destroy him," and he seems to take heart at the example of the city of Dioce or Ecbatan—"4 times was the city re-builded." He courts the end, admitting, "Est consummatum. Ite." He prepares himself for death, remembering all his friends who have died: "Lordly men are to earth o'ergiven / these the companions." He memorializes them all, counting them over:

> Fordie that wrote of giants
> and William who dreamed of nobility
>   and Jim the comedian singing:
>   "Blarrney castle me darlin'
>   you're nothing now but a STOWne"
> and Plarr talking of mathematics.
>   (*LXXIV* 432–33)

But in the end, he refuses the dead-ended life, saying, "I don't know how humanity stands it / with a painted paradise at the end of it / without a painted paradise at the end of it" (*LXXIV* 436). Nothing makes sense to him anymore, even the end. He will not have the end ending, even when he finishes *Canto LXXIV* with the line "we who have passed over Lethe." He begins the next canto with "Out of Phlegethon," addressing Gerhart Munch, the pianist who often played concerts at Rapallo. In *Canto LXXV* he says, "Out of Phlegethon!" "come forth out of Phlegethon," and then Pound copies a choral arrangement that Munch had rewritten for Olga Rudge's violin. Even the end begins to blur or fragment as one passes over Lethe and comes back again out of Phlegethon.

The confusion continues in *Canto LXXVI*, where Pound simply cannot come to any conclusion: "and who's dead, and who isn't / and will the world ever take up its course again?" he asks (*LXXVI* 453). He turns inward to his memories, which accumulate in his solitude at Pisa, admitting that "nothing matters but the quality / of the affection— / in the end—that has carved the trace in the mind / dove sta memoria" (*LXXVI* 457). Knowledge of the end has brought a different test of what matters to Pound. Up to this point he had asked how things worked, not what they mattered. But his condition has changed. He says, "As a lone ant from a broken ant-hill / from the wreckage of Europe, ego scriptor" (*LXXVI* 458). And the broken anthill reminds him that at the end he does not want to add to the wreckage by taking more things apart; rather, he seeks now the unbroken, the indestructible, and he finds it among other places in memories and in the "clouds over the Pisan meadows" "as fine as any to be seen / from the peninsula." Yet such sights cannot sustain the poet for long, and he ends the canto weeping and excusing himself: "States of mind are inexplicable to us" (*LXXVI* 460).

It may well be that states of mind are inexplicable to us, but they also force us to explanations. Out of his sense of desolation and weeping, there comes to Pound the memory of his window in Venice at the turn of the century, and he acknowledges for the first time that "things have ends and beginnings." He repeats this phrase in the next canto, claiming that "things have ends (or scopes) and beginnings." His new knowledge or interest in process leads to the assurance, phrased in a question but nonetheless positively, "How is it far, if you think of it?" That assurance is hard won but essential, and with it Pound has accommodated himself to the end and to a renewed interest in the process by which he has arrived there. He had earlier chastised himself because, when "nothing counts save the quality of the affection," he has had to admit that he had sometimes been a hard man, sympathetic only when it suited his convenience. But once the end itself was sighted, the far made near by being imagined, then he was prepared to go back and summarize the stages of his accomplishments. Here would be a proper ending—a list of what he had achieved.

He says, "To break the pentameter, that was the first heave"

(*LXXXI* 518). Pound had opened to English poetry all other forms of verse—writing himself alliterative verse, sestinas, villanelles, canzones, as well as the free verse of *The Cantos*, and the pentameter too. But the first heave was to free English poetry from its formal restrictions. He then goes on to say: "But to have done instead of not doing / this is not vanity," "To have gathered from the air a live tradition / or from a fine old eye the unconquered flame / This is not vanity. / Here error is all in the not done, / all in the diffidence that faltered" (*LXXXI* 521–22). In the end, it was his vanity, all protestations to the contrary notwithstanding, that saved him. He was consoled finally with the knowledge that "What thou lovest well remains," and what he had loved was the reading and the writing, the gathering and the dissection of texts, the experimentation with forms, the support of his fellow writers.

The Pisan sequence faces the end by gathering into its poems everything that Pound could remember—the memories of the women he loved, the visions that visited him, the accomplishments in which he prided himself, and finally the actual details of the Detention Training Center. The process of writing itself was restorative and consolatory because Pound realized that what had endured the wreckage would endure the end that was to come. In *Canto LXXIV*, Pound talks of the "stone knowing the form which the carver imparts it" (430), and later in *Canto LXXIX* he talks of "the imprint of the intaglio" that depends "in part on what is pressed under it / the mould must hold what is poured into it" (486). Like the stone and the intaglio, Pound himself had held the form. He had come finally to the truth inside discourse which had confronted him at the very beginning of *Poetry Canto I*: "(I stand before the booth, the speech; but the truth / Is inside this discourse—this booth is full of the marrow of wisdom.) / Give up th' intaglio method."

The *Pisan Cantos* are a testimony to Pound's character, to his passion for the written character, to the strength of his curiosity, to the breadth of his interests. He had been wrong, wrong in details and in large programs, but he had not failed in the strength of his literary interests, and it was this quality that finally could sustain the imprint of the intaglio. In the end, he did not give up the intaglio method; he had simply made himself strong enough for it. But the end did not come at Pisa, however closely it approached, and when its presence abated, and Pound was returned to the United States and admitted to St. Elizabeth's Hospital, he went back to his reading and to the subject that had always absorbed his attention—the right use of words.

In *Rock-Drill* and *Thrones*, Pound is concerned with literacy in high office. "Our dynasty came in because of a great sensibility," he opens *Canto LXXXV* (543). The decline of letters and the decline of the state go hand in hand: "No classics, / no American history, / no centre, no general root, / no *prezzo giusto* as core" (549). Much later he writes: "There can be equity in plowing and weeding / when men of war know the Odes. / Esteem sanity in curricula. / You cannot leave out the classics" (*XCIX* 696). Finally, the connection between a right heart, good governance, and literature is established:

> There is worship in plowing
>   and equity in the weeding hoe,
> A field marshal can be literate.
> Might we see it again in our day!
>   7
> All I want is a generous spirit in customs.
>   (*XCIX* 711)

Yet, insistent as he is on literacy, on the classics, and the exact word in these volumes, he is also engaged throughout this period with another aspect of reading—with understanding the signs of nature. At Pisa nature was his primary text, and he said in *Canto LXXXI*, "Learn of the green world what can be thy place / In scaled inventions or true artistry" (521). This interest in the "green world" became important for Pound as he moved far from his own youth and "green world," and it will underpin his final efforts to conclude in *The Drafts and Fragments*. *Canto XC* opens with a quotation from John Heydon's *Holy Guide*, a strange treatise on sympathetic medicine and the use of metals—"From the colour the nature / & by the nature the sign!" Earlier Pound had written:

> "We have", said Mencius, "but phenomena."
> monumenta. In nature are signatures
>   needing no verbal tradition,
> oak leaf never plane leaf. John Heydon.
> . . . .
> In short, the cosmos continues.
>   (*LXXXVII* 573)

Pound's reverence here for the signatures of nature goes back to his earliest ruminations on Imagism and Fenollosa's Chinese written characters when he was chiefly interested in the correspondence between the word and the thing.[17] In contrast, now in these later cantos he seems to be willing to separate the verbal from the natural sign to the prejudice of the former. Unlike the natural tradition, which is clear and exact—"oak leaf never plane leaf"—the verbal tradition is murky, and Pound is urged to repeat Ford Madox Ford's admonition to "get a dictionary / and learn the meaning of words" (*XCVIII* 689). But even with a dictionary, he asks, "Shall two know the same in their knowing?" (*XCIII* 631). He came to put his trust in the cosmos: "In short, the cosmos continues," he says, whereas "the trigger-happy mind," as he calls it in *Canto XCIII*, may or may not continue, and surely its attributes as described here are not fortunate.

At Pisa, learning from the green world as he had to do, Pound took from that world the idea that "it is not man / Made courage, or made order, or made grace." And the thought gave him an undue, but not quite uncharacteristic, appreciation for whatever it was that had made courage, order, and grace. The idea that it was not man who made order must have offered some consolation to a poet harassed by old age and madness and the need to end his poem before the end came.

The recognition in *Thrones* that "cosmos continues," knowledge born of the approaching end, brought him no peace, however. Rather, it threw into relief his own awaiting death and the disorder of his life's project. "From time's wreckage shored, / these fragments shored against ruin," he repeats almost half a century after the Malatesta canto where he had used the words to dissociate himself from Eliot's despair (*CX* 781). Now, ruin at hand, Pound identifies with his old friend, forgetting that he had actually spent his time not shoring fragments but examining them, breaking them down into smaller units, analyzing and dissecting them. The fragment had been Pound's focus of interest until his mind had grown conservative at Pisa. There, immersed in the wreckage, Pound, ever contrary, turned at bay to collect his forces. And in the drafts and fragments of his final years, he seems unable to remember all that he was up to before Pisa, and even some of his consoling thoughts there. "How is it far if you think of it?" he had asked then, imagining that if he could imagine the end he would understand the process. Now he forswears even that vision. "No man can see his own end," Pound says with his own death clearly in view (*CXIII* 787). He was whistling up to the graveyard, claiming with the bravado of old age, "The Gods have not returned. 'They have never left us.'/ They have not returned" (*CXIII* 787).

Remembering now the far past, his own "green time," more clearly than he can recall the interval in between or the present moment, Pound's mind is flooded with his own earliest works. He came to see himself as "A blown husk that is finished" like the wastelanders he had described in *Canto VII*: "Thin husks I had known as men, / Dry casques of departed locusts / speaking a shell of speech . . . / Propped between chairs and table . . . / Words like the locust-shells, moved by no inner being; / A dryness calling for death" (*VII* 26). In his present mood, however, the call for death comes with the conviction that "the light sings

eternal" (*"From CXV"* 794). "Time, space, / neither life nor death
is the answer," he continues, hearing now the siren call of eternity. The contempt of the young man for the thin husks has
deepened into fear, and the fear has engendered a wild hope in
the old man.

But the mind would not let go despite this valedictory, and
Pound turns from the eternally singing light to consider once
again "These concepts the human mind has attained" (*CXVI*
795). It is a strange list:

> To make Cosmos—
> To achieve the possible—
> Muss., wrecked for an error,
> But the record
>   the palimpsest—
> a little light
>   in great darkness—
>   (*CXVI* 795)

One line is undercut by the next, the Cosmos disintegrating into
the great darkness by stages, checked by the "possible," by the
"record," "a little light," but moving nonetheless toward disorder and chaos. Or perhaps the reader alone moves them in
that direction, since the lines or words do not form any grammatical unit. As he often does, Pound leaves the phrases incomplete, and the appositions without clear relationships.

Pound tries again to say what he has attained, casting about
for parallels and discovering "Justinian's / a tangle of works unfinished." That image calls up its opposite: "I have brought the
great ball of crystal; / who can lift it? / Can you enter the great
acorn of light?" Pound's mind is still working in antithetical
ways: the codification of laws and the great ball of crystal, like
the nineteen-year-long evidence for the first case and the splendor of splendors. The two opposing models of *The Cantos* remained in Pound's consciousness to the very end, even when he
felt he had failed miserably at both. And his final gesture was to

point to these models just beyond or in back of the poem: "i.e. it coheres all right / even if my notes do not cohere," and "A little light, like a rushlight / to lead back to splendour" (*CXVI* 797).

Pound grew old in *The Cantos*, and if in the final drafts he forgot what he was actually about, there remained to him nonetheless certain familiar habits of mind. The concepts the human mind had attained were difficult to summon up; but the conceptualizing habits held fast. The "mind as Ixion, unstill, ever turning," he says (*CXIII* 790). To the very end, Pound continued to offer statement and counterstatement in order to release the lurking distinction, "man seeking good, / doing evil," or in order to manipulate the rhetorical surprise of transferred terms, "where the dead walked / and the living were made of cardboard" (*CXV* 794), or simply to bring proverbial contrasting pairs together, "Many errors, / a little rightness" (*CXVI* 797). He continued to claim and probably to believe that he was doing something that he was not doing; for example, "I tried to make a paradiso / terrestre" ("Notes for CXVII *et seq.*" 802). This plan, ambiguously either political or literary, does not square with Pound's eagerness to unmake, to dissect, to collate.

Pound's profoundly contradictory nature endured to the end. He liked the "Vision of the Madonna / above the cigar butts" (*CXVI* 795), the ideal against the real. He moved his poem forward both here and throughout *The Cantos* by bringing together divisive elements, by taking them apart. He imagined he had not been able to make the poem cohere when, in fact, he had never tried. He had a genius for fragmenting lines, words, concepts, documents. Here again, as in the *Pisan Cantos*, he writes about the end in open form, acknowledging finality by denying its form. Such habits of mind kept *The Cantos* open when the interpretation of history that underpinned them might have—indeed should have— caused the poem to come to a halt. The mind that loved Douglas's economic theories had to be checked and disturbed by the other mind, which was almost usurious in the value it could create from other texts.

Finally, Pound's concern was "And as to who will copy this palimpsest?" (*CXVI* 797). He could not accept the end, despite the splendor he saw before him, without imagining a new Pound, another chance. The person he seeks is his own younger self, the reader of texts, the spectator he left in *Poetry Canto I* outside the diorama booth, imagining the truth inside discourse. To such a person, he has bequeathed the "errors and wrecks" that lie about him, the notes that "do not cohere," "Many errors, / a little rightness"; in short he has left for his future reader the unfinished work with instructions on how to read it. Then he swerves, as if he hoped to claim more for himself, provide a new guide for his readers, show them how to finish the text: "But to affirm the gold thread in the pattern" (*CXVI* 797). The infinitive looks both ways, backward to his own ambition and forward to his hopes for his readers, but it is wishful thinking in either direction. To "affirm the gold thread" in the weave of *The Cantos* is both to set the right value on gold and to appreciate Pound's own judgment in the matter. The phrase looks back to the usury canto: "None learneth to weave gold in her pattern" (*LXV* 230). Pound explains this line in a letter by claiming that in the Middle Ages in Rapallo actual gold thread was woven into the cloth (SL 304). With usury, such practices had ceased. He had admired those who wove the gold thread in the pattern, but he had been aware of those who had stopped the weaving, making "Aurum est commune sepulchrum," for example (*XLVI* 234–35). Pound testifies here to the rightness of his own principles and to their continuity in the pattern that is his poem. Beyond that, he makes a claim for those parts of the cantos that are like "a little rightness," "A little light," the points of greatest value and illumination.

As to his readers, what pattern can they find when he himself admits to ample wrecks? But, of course, that is precisely the point of reading. Pound is putting his readers perhaps consciously, but certainly with a greater shrewdness than the weariness of this canto might indicate, exactly in the position from which he started: outside the booth, looking in, anxious to get the inside out and bombarded with contradictory ideas about how to do it. If reading were simply a copying of the palimpsest or only an affirmation of the figure in the carpet, it would be a task easily assignable to clerks or to particularly sensitive geometricians. But reading is something beyond this passive copying and active affirming, as Pound himself had discovered in a lifetime.

For Pound, reading had always been an essentially antagonistic activity. He sought out adversarial texts, written in languages remote and difficult or from motives intentionally perverse or by people obscured in time. He read what he did not quite understand, understood what he had not quite read, because reading, as he practised it, was an endlessly creative act of dissection and reconstruction, of turning the inside out and the outside in, of honoring the space between the reader and the read. There is always a margin in the texts Pound read and finally in the text he had written, since his writing no less than his reading was antagonistic. And it was never more so than in his last days, when he turned to read his own text and direct his reader in the reading. It was not the work he had hoped to write, he seems to say, but he had offered no clear idea of such a work either early or late. Just as at the beginning with all before him, Pound could wonder, "What's left for me to do?" so at the end with the colossus behind him, he could refer to it as "a little rightness," "A little light." He is protesting, apologizing, despairing, obviously both in the beginning and at the end. By leaving the text open, he closed it splendidly: a little light after all "to lead back to splendour." Because he loved the fragment and the ruin and built his poem both by and on fragments, tearing down completed structures including his own work in progress, he kept the work before him, always leaving something to do. His final gesture to his readers was to place them in the position he was about to vacate.

6 *Conclusion*

THE MODERNIST LONG POEM is not a genre but an aspiration to
form that may have had an experimental beginning but could
not escape its conservative end. In its long development, the history of American Modernism can be traced. In a way un-
suspected by Williams, the beginning was assuredly the end,
because embedded in the desire to write a long poem is an
idealization of form, a conservative will that must check every
experiment against its ambition to length. If American Modernism can be understood by what the major poets wrote, then its
history is the history of the long public poem, of each poet's long
attempt to write it, and of the succession of such efforts by different poets over almost half a century.[1]

The long poem became for each of these different poets a
turning away from an earlier commitment to forms that were
essentially borrowed from European avant-garde writing, if in

fact one can write imitative avant-garde work. Despite flashes of surrealism in *The Waste Land* or of futurism in *The Bridge*, for example, the long poem was a movement beyond the avant-garde tendencies of early Modernism. In starting *The Cantos*, Pound abandoned the antirepresentational bias of vorticism, just as Williams moved away from the Dadaist tendencies of *Spring & All* in *Paterson*.

A second stage of creative activity, the long poem for the American Modernists was an effort to imagine an original form; it was not avant-garde but rather simply garde—that is, a form for containing, watching, admonishing. But in this imagining, the avant-garde cult of the new was not entirely obliterated.[2] The concept itself recurs in the Modernists' work: in Pound's "Make it new," Crane's "New verities, new inklings," Williams' "to break / through the skull of custom." The new as avant-garde—as an active and antagonistic movement against the traditional—was linked for the American Modernist poet in a way not fully acknowledged to something not new, but renewed or restored, and so not antagonistic. For example, "Invent (if you can) discover or / nothing is clear," is the advice given to the poet in Williams' poem. He means that term *invent* both in its modern meaning of making something new as well as in its archaic meaning of discovering what is already there and renewing it. It also has the implications of its Latin root, which means coming upon or coming into.

The new as the world renewed in and by the long poem is one project that the American Modernists took over from the Romantics. But the Modernists' intention to write poems about the city and its history set them apart from the Romantics, and the choice of subject itself offered a certain resistance to their creative efforts. Antagonistic to the restorative imagination, the city as a subject required novelties of expression that have come to be considered the defining gesture of Modernism. The extent to which these new forms were efforts to make old subjects new and new conditions responsive to traditional values has remained obscure in discussions of Modernism that concentrate on its formal experimentation.

This examination of the long poem's composition has revealed that poems which may seem to be intentional experiments with form were often compromises with the poet's original intentions that were made in the writing, rather than deliberate initial objectives. For example, the discontinuous form of *The Waste Land*, admittedly there from the start of the poem's composition, was intensified by Eliot's revision of purpose and Pound's editorial advice. It was not so much an experiment with form as a reconciliation to mixed form by a poet anxious to put into some kind of final arrangement a long poem. It emerged from Eliot's early slavish imitation of eighteenth-century models, his random casting about for some line that would sustain development. The poem's discontinuous form was an experiment, but also a concession to an incomplete and uncertain process of revision in which Eliot aimed at greater continuity in the poem.

Eliot's case is significant because his was the most contracted period of composition, and thus offered the greatest possibility for realizing the experiment in form he intended to make, if indeed he had such an intention. But the evidence suggests that at the start he had no idea of the form his poem would take. Thus, *The Waste Land*, for all its novelty, is not properly an avant-garde experiment in form but rather a hesitant movement to conserve in one form as much as the poet had written. In contrast to Eliot, Pound took half a century to compose *The Cantos* and so produced the barrier of time against any initiating idea of experimentation. Yet curiously enough *The Cantos* has a greater consistency of experimental form—the organization by canto, the allusiveness, the mixture of lyric interludes and didactic moments, the multi-languagedness, the radical fragmentation of the text—than *The Waste Land*. Clearly, Pound's idea of how to invent in poetry developed and was reconceived as he wrote throughout the hazards of a long creative career; but he never renovated his original experiment with form, and as he wrote it eventually became a convention.

Eliot and Pound provide good and opposing examples to consider in estimating the invention of Modernism. Eliot gained his form by a piecemeal process of composition that had no clear intention. Pound maintained his form despite every insight he might have had in the writing. He made it new and then he remade it and remade it. Intention may not be the sole requirement of invention, however, and the poets' foundering intentions to make it new need not preclude the possibility that, however haphazard the compositon, the long poem is a radically new construction. The Modernist long poem appears to be such a work, and yet, in every example studied here, the desire to invent as well as discover was tested and checked by the writing, and the poem emerged in a contest between the poet's initial experiment and what he found he could actually write. The composition of the long poem served to provide these poets with a sense of the limits of invention, of language, and of the power of the imagination, and so disappointed many avant-garde hopes. As the poets came to realize these limits toward the end of their poems, they grew anxious to conserve what they could within them. They were as reluctant to end the poem as to extend the limits.

More important, the long poem was not avant-garde in its content. Its experiment in form did not emerge from new materials in any organic scheme of development, but was laid over rather conventional concepts. For example, Pound's novel and playful use of the written character by translation, appropriation, and fragmentation, is tied to a nineteenth-century ethic of character that is unitary and originary, an ethic that itself derived from ancient origins, as Pound admits in *Canto XIII*: "And Kung said, 'Without character you will / be unable to play on that instrument / Or to execute the music fit for the Odes'" (*XIII* 60). Or Williams, imagining that he was searching for a form never before imagined, yearned to reveal with it not worlds unknown but the most ancient concept of the *genius loci*, "that secret and sacred presence," buried in the modern city. It was perhaps a world unknown, but unknown only in the conditions of the modern world and recoverable under certain conditions. And Crane, who would "set breath to steel" and celebrate "Easters of speeding light," tied the new conditions of the machine age not to "new verities" but to the familiar project of the sublime, new here only as it is assimilated to technology, and then not entirely new but reminiscent of Whitman.

The program, Williams' and Crane's no less than Pound's, was to restore, to lift up, to instruct, and to improve a world judged totally degraded. But the poet was to remain responsive to that world; his creative opportunities were in it. Williams' lament— "As Carrie Nation / to Artemis / so is our life today"—was no cause for turning away from that history, but a determination to reverse its ratio. In choosing the city and its history as subjects, the long poem called into question its status as a Modernist work. Paul de Man points to the "radical impulse that stands behind all genuine modernity," "moments at which all anteriority vanishes, annihilated by the power of an absolute forgetting," that would appear to make modernity and history diametrically opposed to each other.[3] Thus, he claims, the appeal of modernity is its rejection of history, although history itself gives literature its own duration.

Modernist / long / poetry—each term, as the poets understood it, subverted the others. The poem can be long and experimental only by plan or intention; in this it resembles prose. Thus, it must deny its place as the first language, as a spontaneous form of expression, and it must deny too the gifts that can come from inspiration and irrational modes of association. Also, the poem can only be about history by limiting its experimental opportunities, rejecting its rejection of history and thus its modernity.

The effort to hold in balance these contradictions suggests the extent to which the complex form of the Modernist long poem and the movement that it came to define are conservative in impulse, permissive in allowing as much as possible to be conserved, but not revolutionary. Poem and movement succeeded by a generous allowance. The extended poem and period of the Modernist movement had a continuity that ultimately confirmed the history and temporality that both appeared initially committed to question or reject. Even, for example, the imagistic opening of *Paterson*, which presents momentarily a new world, a world made new by the "power of an absolute forgetting," serves actually to restore in the embrace of the man-city and woman-flower the whole history of industrialization. It took Williams almost the full writing of the poem to *discover* this truth, and he did not like it once it was discovered, but by then it had become the subject of his poem. To find in the city's history the moment before history, the beginning, Williams had to forswear the revolution that he wanted and conserve all that he hoped to reject. His poem added up, and like Pound, at the end he was struck with its weight. It became for him the Book of Lead, not entirely unlike Pound's quite dissimilar image, "the great ball of crystal."

The commodiousness of these Modernist poetic experiments, which allowed both varied forms and varied materials, appeared at first to be a new conception of form, open and responsive to the new conditions of modernity. But as it developed, the poem became more settled in its attitude. The burden of the long poem, pressing against its subjects, developed into satire, but satire without much laughter or mockery and written by poets more anxious to instruct and judge than to humor or cajole. And in this mode, the movement from *The Waste Land* to *The Cantos* is toward an increasingly self-conscious, despairing, and conservative end.

The restoration of *The Waste Land* is to fertility, and in this the poem demonstrates ties with the origins of satire in magic, in efforts to drive away evil influences in order to release sexual potency. There is a kind of suppressed raucousness in the poem, an expansive embrace of the world's variety that is lacking from *Paterson* and evident only in the early hell cantos of Pound. Madame Sosostris at one end and Mr. Eugenides at the other offer up a banquet of bawdy tastes. Eliot's effort to uncover the energies submerged and degraded in these characters points to a more radical transformation than Crane's pronouncement for "new thresholds, new anatomies." Crane's unitary vision cannot be new because it exists always outside of time. Despite its affirmations, *The Bridge* is ultimately lifeless. When it descends from its soaring into the world, it finds only "highsteppers," "the persuasive suburban land agent," subjects so degraded that they can elicit only the poet's sneers and sarcasm. The citizens of Crane's poetic universe are degraded beyond his imaginative power to restore them, and inaccurately he attributed the fault to them. But it was the poet himself who lacked the sympathy that might have given his mockery the force of restitution.

Tied as it is to the particular, *Paterson* is tied to the conservation of each particular, and thus to the final engorgement that Williams details in *Paterson V*: "The (self) direction has been changed / the serpent / its tail in its mouth / 'the river has returned to its beginnings' / and backward / (and forward) / it tortures itself within me / until time has been washed finally under" (P 233). The Gnostic serpent with its tail in its mouth had fascinated Williams since *Spring & All*, where he wrote: "Emptiness stares us once more in the face. . . . Has life its tail in its mouth or its mouth in its tail?" (S&A 14). In *Paterson*, he returns to this alchemical allegory of devouring to express his ambiguous relation to a world he had hoped to revive. The metamorphosis of bad into good, good into bad, had tipped in favor of the bad by the time Williams concluded his poem.

And *The Cantos*, more dependent than any other poem on history because more lengthy, more steeped in its own history, thins out eventually into the despair, "That I lost my center / fighting the world. / The dreams clash / and are shattered"

("Notes for CXVII *et seq.*" 802). Pound's antagonism is not avant-garde but ante-garde; it comes from a desire to fight the world into shape, to make it accord with an ideal, to center it in his imagination. In this, Pound is the most reactionary and dejected of the Modernists. His appeal to "Cosmos" in the end is an appeal beyond history, a conservative hope or rather a hope to conserve, elicited from a deepened sense of how much he has destroyed. Like Crane, Pound would have "Answerer of all" or he would have nothing.

From the satire of *The Waste Land* to the reactionary fulminations of *The Cantos*, Modernism would appear to witness a dwindling of creative energies, and yet, a movement that started in an aspiration to form could hope for no fuller expression than *The Cantos, Paterson, The Bridge, The Waste Land*. This achievement of form was tied to a mastery of content, or at least to an increasingly fuller confrontation with the problems of representation and referentiality. Here, Eliot's task was simplest because earliest and thus more shockingly iconoclastic. His experimental mixture of realism and surrealism could not be repeated without acknowledging its compromises and admitting its paradoxical dependence and imitations. But as the discussions of Crane and Williams have suggested, to move beyond Eliot was a move toward the problematic confrontation with referentiality. It is this insistence on referentiality that differentiates American Modernism from its European and English roots, as Yeats pointed out over fifty years ago, when, in his introduction to the *Oxford Book of Modern Verse*, he argued that there were two contrasting kinds of modern poetry—the poetry of representation and poetry that would no longer be mimetic. Yeats' condemnation of the first need not interest us here so much as his identification of Pound and Eliot with it. He might also have included Williams and Crane as representative Americans.

The American wing of Modernism is distinguished, then, not only by its aspiration to form but by the interest in representation that fired it. And not simply representation but instruction.

Unlike Baudelaire, the American Modernists found no heresy in didacticism. They would not agree with him that poetry has no object but itself and is written solely for the pleasure of writing a poem.[4] Still, their ambivalence toward representation took various forms. Eliot's "Unreal city" is Baudelaire's "*Fourmillante cité*," *and* "King William Street." Crane's Brooklyn Bridge is fact *and* symbol, there between Wall Street and the Atlantic Ocean and also "harp and altar, of the fury fused."

This oscillation between the city in reality and the city in poetry indicates the extent to which the long poem retained some vestiges of the lyric's retreat into irreality even when its ambition was to public discourse. Baudelaire's aspiration to lose the real was not shared by the American Modernists even when they did share his sense of the confinement of reality and the depersonalization of art. The difficulty, even obscurity, of the modern lyric has been attributed to its nonreferentiality; but the difficulty of the long poem is precisely in its referentiality, its attempt to renew that referentiality, not to purify it by removing it from public discourse, but to reattach it to public meaning. Thus, for example, the Brooklyn Bridge had to become in Crane's poem not just a convenient way across the harbor but a modern invention of bridgeship, of linkage, and of connections. And Williams, in observing the falls above Paterson, attempted over and over again to make them refer to language itself: "the roar, / the roar of the present, a speech— / is, of necessity, my sole concern" (P 144).

The subject of the poem, the insistence on subject, then produced its own dilemma of form because, committed to referentiality, the long poem was equally committed to its power of purification and restoration. Williams, who had the most particular subject of all these poets, had also the most persistent problems in identifying it. He claims to have taken "the city as my 'case' to work up, really to work it up" (P viii); but his difficulties were always with its content. It is not that he could not work up a case; it is rather that the case he could make never coincided with the idea or the poem he imagined. As he turned to celebrate the world, he was more repelled by it than attracted, more driven to censure than to praise, and the long poem that was designed to accommodate his reception of the world came eventually to express a disgruntled rejection, and only at the end an attachment, by then sentimental and false. The poem's open form was inconsistent from the start with Williams' desire to diagnose and cure. If the referentiality of *Paterson* was the undoing of Williams' ambitions, it came to be the doing of his poem.

From *The Waste Land* to *The Cantos*, the long poem moved toward a greater concern for its status as a public poem. Its longer form and more extended period of composition allowed a more expanded engagement with the subject and consequently a greater self-reflexivity about the poem's ambition to public stature. But if Modernism is a movement of long public poems, what is a public poem written in an age when the term had only a derogatory connotation, and by poets who imagined that they looked out over the "last cess-pool of the universe," "The slough of unamiable liars" (*XIV* 62–63)? The public poem would have an uneasy subject. The poem's public status could justify the poem's fragmented form on the basis that fragmented is imitative form, as John Addington Symonds argues in his *Studies of the Greek Poets*, which Williams quotes in *Paterson*: "the Greeks displayed their acute aesthetic sense of propriety, recognizing the harmony which subsists between crabbed verse and the distorted subjects with which they deal—the vices and perversions of humanity—as well as their agreement with the snarling spirit of the satirist. Deformed verse is suited to deformed morality" (P 40). Thus the poet could throw onto his public subjects the responsibility of form.

But if the public itself produced the snarls and thus could account for the spirit, it did not make the writing of the Modernist long poem simple. Eliot, who started out to write satire, found it difficult to do, or rather he found that it did not express either the full range of his experience or the central need of his imagination, and he abandoned it early. The public status of *The Waste Land* could not justify its discontinuous form as mimetic because, despite Eliot's later admission, the poem was not simply a personal grouse against the conditions of his own life or the conditions of his world. Like the long poems it was to inspire, *The Waste Land* was a positive appeal to virtue and to the restoration of the poet as its arbiter. This impulse behind the poem forced the poet to acknowledge his own inadequacies and drove Eliot at least to search for support outside the poem in cultural anthropology. Inside the poem, he was tormented by his inability to master his materials and to gain a public control over his private anguish.

Eliot was only the first to confront this issue, and in every poem the poet as a writer of public poems becomes a central concern. Part of what remained to be restored was the poet himself. Eliot plays with the idea of the maddened poet courted, as he is abused, by the mad world, in his allusions to a whole tradition of such figures from Arnaut Daniel to Hieronymo at the end of *The Waste Land*. In this, Eliot is closer to the avant-garde notion of the alienated poet than is Crane, for example, whose experience may have been alienated but who held firm to the poet as a spokesman for the public. Crane is much more conventional than Eliot, despite the frenzied pitch of his poem. And yet, paradoxically, the allusiveness of *The Waste Land* suggests how firmly Eliot depended on the poet as the spokesman for his age, for all ages. To restore the poet was to restore the divine sense of his madness. The poet in *The Waste Land*, the poet restored to the wasteland, is a complicated figure: not the individual talent placed in tradition, but alternately the avant-garde artist and the prophet.

Crane, who composed in fits of inspiration and was always subject to bouts of alcoholism or depression, distances that madness in his portrait of the poet. His aim was to restore the poet as shaman, as explorer committed to journey for the public, the poet as "Falcon-Ace": "Thou hast there in thy wrist a Sanskrit charge / To conjugate infinity's dim marge— / Anew!" Or again, as "floating singer," the poet is adrift in the world, but spokesman for a vision beyond it: "(O Thou whose radiance doth inherit me)." For Crane, the poet was commissioned by a public, duty-bound to its service, not alien but its chief citizen. Eliot's irony and his mockery both of the poet's pretensions and the world's inadequacies are flattened out in Crane's bland and innocent acceptance of those very qualities.

Williams' opening identification as "just another dog / among a lot of dogs" (P 3) would appear to allow the poet only the most degraded public personality. But none of these poets was more self-conscious than Williams, more willing to try on a variety of roles, to be self-deprecating and self-vaunting—in short, to pose. He is in turn a fellow sufferer, as alienated from the world as any man he meets, announcer of the "Beautiful thing," a student himself of the world's lesson that "Virtue is wholly / in the effort to be virtuous," and above all an instructor with a series of earnest pronouncements from "No ideas but in things" to "no woman is virtuous / who does not give herself to her lover / —forthwith" (P 229). He remained aloof from a public he judged as inane who could ask: "How *do* / you find the time for it in // your busy life?" (P 114). Or he patronized his audience: "Geeze, Doc, I guess it's all right / but what the hell does it mean?" No alienated poet in Eliot's style, Williams suffered nonetheless a profound disgust for his townspeople that gave to his public poem a regrettable moralistic overtone, or perhaps more accurately Williams simply assumed the poetic counterpart of the doctor's paternal attitude. This attitude corrupted the poet.

Pound early carved out for himself a central role as the poet who would be the spokesman of his age, a public poet. Maddened though he was and tortured beyond endurance by a public who neither read nor valued him, Pound was concerned early and late with the figure of the poet as a political power.

The Cantos are full of advisors to kings, more successful than Pound himself, but always urging the restoration of the books. He recounts one exchange between leader and noble envoy: "to whom KAO: I conquered the empire on horseback. / to whom Lou: Can you govern it in that manner?" (*LIV* 276).

The exercise of power depended always upon the power of knowledge. Brute force, even directed against himself, was never so terrifying to Pound as not knowing the words. His advice was always: "get a dictionary / and learn the meaning of words" (*XCVIII* 689). Philology and poetry, his two interests, then were the underpinnings of his public stature. They have often been considered opposites, one tied to the text's and the world's objectivity and referentiality and the other committed to itself and to a radical subjectivity. For Pound, however, they combined to affirm his double confidence in the world and in himself. The private act of reading, the public act of writing, allowed him to announce in his poem: "This is not a work of fiction / nor yet of one man" (*XCIX* 708). Despite his preposterous claims, Pound is earnest here, and it is his sincerity that indicates his obtuseness. No man but Pound could have written *The Cantos*; it is emphatically the work of *one* man despite its allusions and quotations. In no other poem studied here has the quixotic taste of the poet so dominated the materials. Yet, as tormented as Le Prince d'Aquitaine, Pound can still claim, "But the beauty is not the madness" (*CXVI* 795).

Pound did restore the poet to the public view but in no way that would bring him honor. His trial and sentencing to imprisonment, his years at St. Elizabeth's Hospital for the Criminally Insane, his widely publicized release, all these extraliterary means brought Pound into the public in a way that his poetry had denied him. In a way, he is the public poet of his generation, far outpacing Eliot, whose critical tastes dominated the age; Crane, who hoped to be its Whitman; and Williams, who lived in the public as a doctor and tried to embrace the local world in which he lived. It was Pound's notoriety, not his poetry, that first made him a public figure.

The idea of the public poet and the public poem dominated American Modernism and makes it impossible to define the movement, as Lionel Trilling has done, as anticultural, antisocial, and subversive.[5] Trilling draws his conclusions from *Heart of Darkness, Death in Venice, Notes from Underground, The Death of Ivan Ilytch,* and *The Magic Mountain,* and with that European tradition he has a point. But the modern element in American Modernist poetry is deeply cultural, social, and restorative. The split cannot be attributed to the difference between prose and poetry—one rational and thus modern, the other spontaneous and thus ancient—because the qualities that Trilling assigns to prose are those traditionally assigned to poetry.[6] For Trilling, Modernist prose is antirational, elevating the unconscious above the conscious, passion over reason. And by contrast, American Modernist poetry has or longs for a public status that would have to depend on reason and conscious intention, traditionally prosaic qualities. If not between prose and poetry, then perhaps the split comes between European and American expressions of Modernism, especially since European Modernist poetry could have been used to support Trilling's argument. That point has been conceded already, but it undermines the internationalization of literature that Modernism has been credited with introducing.[7]

What then *is* Modernism in American poetry? It is, at its most inclusive, a movement that started with a radical rejection of the conditions of modern life and developed into an awareness of its own limits, a nostalgic regret at such knowledge, and a retrospective appeal over it to a better knowledge. It was, from start to finish, conservative in the sense that it aimed to conserve and to destroy only in order to conserve. Its deepest impulse was an affirmative one, but one tested by time and tempered by disappointment. Modernism, insofar as it is represented in the long poem, is no movement that Lionel Trilling would recognize, because it is deeply implicated in the culture that it surveyed and judged. But Trilling's assessment of Modernism is in itself a product of its place and time, and so perhaps not appropriate for this later day.

Again, what is American Modernism? It is the long writing of the long poem.

Notes

1. Introduction

1. Ricardo J. Quinones traces four stages of growth in the Modernist movement, starting with its avant-garde phase, and developing toward more positive expressions of its new consciousness into a mythopoetic art and finally to a pullback toward history, in *Mapping Literary Modernism: Time and Development* (Princeton: Princeton University Press, 1985). Quinones is concerned with time as a theme in Modernism, and his main focus is quite different from mine. However, his book will corroborate my own understanding of Modernism as a movement with an important development.

2. For a discussion of these poems as a sequence of lyrical moments, see M. L. Rosenthal and Sally M. Gall, *The Modern Poetic Sequence: The Genius of Modern Poetry* (New York: Oxford University Press, 1983). Considering the lyric poem as the paradigm of modernity is more accurate in French, German, and English poetry than in American poetry. Paul de Man discusses the problematic identifi-

cation of the lyric and modernity in *Blindness and Insight: Essays in the Rhetoric of Contemporary Criticism* (New York: Oxford University Press, 1971), 166–86.

3. Joseph Frank, "Spatial Form in Modern Literature," in *The Widening Gyre: Crisis and Mastery in Modern Literature* (Bloomington: Indiana University Press, 1968), 13.

4. Ezra Pound, *"Paris Review Interview,"* in Donald Hall, ed., *Remembering Poets: Reminiscences and Opinions* (New York: Harper Colophon Books, 1977), 241.

5. A study of the long poem from Spenser to Pound and including chapters on Eliot and Pound, which I read after I had finished my own work, is Balachandra Rajan's *The Form of the Unfinished: English Poetics from Spenser to Pound* (Princeton: Princeton University Press, 1985). He traces the history of the unfinished poem to an environment of indeterminacy in which the unfinished assumes its formal prominence. Rajan finds in Pound and Eliot a contest between the poem's fragmentary method and its holistic objective.

2. *The Waste Land*

1. Hugh Kenner, "The Urban Apocalypse," in A. Walton Litz, ed., *Eliot in His Time* (Princeton: Princeton University Press, 1973), 47. I am indebted throughout my discussion to Kenner's comments.

2. Helen Gardner argues that Eliot was writing against the natural bent of his genius in trying to keep to a manner or style that was not natural to him. See *"The Waste Land*: Paris 1922," in *Eliot in His Time*, 92.

3. Kenner identifies the example of Dryden behind Eliot's first conception of *The Waste Land*. See his discussion in *Eliot in His Time*, 25–34.

4. *"The Paris Review Interview*: T. S. Eliot," in Donald Hall, *Remembering Poets*, "Appendix," 211.

5. The repetitions here and elsewhere in *The Waste Land* suggest that this method of concentration was available to Eliot even in the poem's synthetic method and was not, as Charles Altieri argues, a method developed only in "Ash Wednesday." The act of mind in

The Waste Land is more complicated than Altieri suggests in his
provocative essay "Objective Image and Act of Mind in Modern
Poetry," *PMLA* 91 (January 1976): 101–14.

6. For an account of Eliot's creative use of the thunder's command,
   see William Harmon, "T. S. Eliot's Raids on the Inarticulate,"
   PMLA 91 (May 1976): 450–67.

7. Here I differ from my conclusions in an earlier article. See Margaret Dickie Uroff, "*The Waste Land*: Metatext," *The Centennial
   Review* 24 (Spring 1980): 148–66.

8. Jessie L. Weston, *From Ritual to Romance* (New York: Anchor
   Books, 1957), 188.

9. See Eliot's review "Ulysses, Order and Myth," *The Dial* 75
   (November 1923): 480–83.

10. Kenner, "The Urban Apocalypse," 47.

11. For a full discussion of this doubleness in *The Waste Land*, see
    Robert Langbaum, "New Modes of Characterization in *The Waste
    Land*," in *Eliot in His Time*, 95–128.

3. *The Bridge*

1. See the letter to Otto Kahn, March 18, 1926, which outlines the
   poem and explains the "interlocking elements and symbols at
   work" in the poem, in LHC, 240–42. The critical debate over *The
   Bridge* goes back to its early reviewers—Allen Tate and Yvor Winters, among others—who had praised Crane's first volume of poetry, *White Buildings*, but found *The Bridge* a failure. See Tate's
   "Hart Crane," in *Reactionary Essays on Poetry and Ideas* (New York:
   Charles Scribner's Sons, 1936), 26–42, and Winters, "The Progress of Hart Crane," *Poetry* 36 (June 1930): 153–65. The discussion continues in John Unterecker's "The Architecture of *The
   Bridge*," *Wisconsin Studies in Contemporary Literature* 3 (Spring–
   Summer 1962): 5–20; Donald Pease's "Blake, Crane, Whitman,
   and Modernism: A Poetics of Pure Possibility," *PMLA* 96 (Janu-
   ary 1981): 64–85; Suzanne Clark Doeren, "Theory of Culture,
   Brooklyn Bridge, and Hart Crane's Rhetoric of Memory," *MMLA
   Bulletin* 15 (Spring 1982): 18–28.

2. Joseph Riddel, "Hart Crane's Poetics of Failure," *ELH* 33 (December 1966): 482.

3. R. W. B. Lewis, "Days of Wrath and Laughter," in *Trials of the Word* (New Haven: Yale University Press, 1965), 202.

4. See the drafts of "Atlantis" in Brom Weber, *Hart Crane* (New York: The Bodley Press, 1948), Appendix C, 425–40.

5. Weber, 432–33.

6. Weber, 437.

7. R. W. B. Lewis makes this point in *The Poetry of Hart Crane* (Princeton: Princeton University Press, 1967), 265.

8. Lewis, 311–12.

9. See Eric J. Sundquist, "Bringing Home the Word: Magic, Lies, and Silence in Hart Crane," *ELH* 44 (Summer 1977): 376–99, for a psychoanalytic reading of this passage and the whole poem. Sundquist reads the poem as the story of "the sacrifice of ancestral fathers with one eye toward sexual reunion with a maternal, *free* origin, the other toward the *debt* aroused by the parricide necessary to an acquisition of power over that origin" (376).

10. Crane's fascination with names and puns is discussed by John Irwin, "Naming Names: Hart Crane's 'Logic of Metaphor,'" *The Southern Review* 11 (April 1975): 284–99, and by Roger Ramsey, "A Poetics for *The Bridge*," *Twentieth Century Literature* 26 (Fall 1980): 278–93.

11. John Carlos Rowe develops the Nietzschean bias in Crane's treatment of history in "The 'Super-Historical' Sense of Hart Crane's *The Bridge*," *Genre* 11 (Winter 1978): 597–625.

4. *Paterson*

1. It is this Williams for whom everything exists not only in the beginning but in every succeeding moment that J. Hillis Miller sets at the summit of twentieth-century poetry in *Poets of Reality* (New York: Atheneum, 1969).

2. F. Douglass Fiero traces the beginning back to the eighty-five-line poem "Paterson," published in 1927. See "Williams Creates the First Book of *Paterson*," *Journal of Modern Literature* 3 (1974): 965–86.

3. In "William Carlos Williams' *Paterson*," *Sagetrieb* 1 (Spring 1982): 13–47, M. L. Rosenthal and Sally M. Gall consider *Paterson* as a sequence of varied lyrical moments put together as a collage

might be constructed. But they neglect the anxieties Williams expresses here, anxieties explained in part by Margaret L. Bollard, who suggests that Williams finally organized the poem by interlacing the material he had amassed. See "The Interlace Element in *Paterson*," *Twentieth Century Literature* 21 (October 1975): 288–304.

4. William Carlos Williams papers at Beinecke Library, Yale University, 185–88.

5. See Paul Mariani, *William Carlos Williams: A New World Naked* (New York: McGraw-Hill Book Co., 1981), 414. Mariani calls this passage the core of *Paterson* (581–84).

6. Joseph Riddel has argued that Williams' poetics brings into question the New Critical idea of art as autotelic or as an incarnation of either the Word or consciousness. He sees Williams' "radiant gist" not as another metaphor for presence but as the name of a function like Derrida's *supplément*—undetermined overabundance, dissonance. Riddel views Williams as a post-Modernist who is anxious to destroy the Book and with it the view of literature as a Text or Word with a total meaning, in order to make writing possible once more. But he fails to take into account Williams' repeated statement that he wanted to embody the knowable world, that he had the whole of *Paterson* in his mind from the start and had but to fill in the details, that he entertained this dream of the whole poem.

7. For a biographical treatment of *Paterson V*, see Paul Mariani, "*Paterson* 5: The Whore/Virgin and the Wounded One-Horned Beast," *Denver Quarterly* 13 (Summer 1978): 102–30.

5. *The Cantos*

1. An unpublished letter in the D. D. Paige collection, Beinecke Library, Yale University.

2. Ronald Bush, *The Genesis of Ezra Pound's Cantos* (Princeton: Princeton University Press, 1976), reprints the *Poetry Cantos* from which I quote in the following pages.

3. Bush comments on the ways in which Pound responded to Browning's self-reflexivity, taking over his experiments with narrative form, making the narrator a character in his own story,

portraying the way an action acquires significance in an individual intelligence. See Bush, 76–87.

4. See Bush on the influence of Joyce and Eliot, 183–255.

5. Letter to Isabel Pound, November 1, 1924, Paige collection, Beinecke.

6. Daniel Pearlman, *The Barb of Time* (New York: Oxford University Press, 1969), Appendix A, 302.

7. Pearlman, 303.

8. See Donald Davie's account of the similarity between Pound's method and that of William Carlos Williams' *In The American Grain*, where Williams boasts: "I copied and used the original writings. . . . I did this with malice aforethought to prove the truth of my book, since the originals fitted into it without effort on my part, perfectly, leaving not a seam." *Ezra Pound: Poet as Sculptor* (New York: Oxford University Press, 1964), 124–25.

9. Carroll Terrell, *A Companion to the Cantos of Ezra Pound* (Berkeley: University of California Press, 1980), 81. Pound translated the word as "and pain ameises," following Levy's suggestion. See "Arnaut Daniel," in Ezra Pound, In, 313. In this passage in *The Cantos*, Pound does not give Levy's translation, leaving the whole matter unresolved by conjuring up a scene similar to Arnaut's quasi-allegorical tree of love, not a direct translation of that scene but a contiguous landscape with "Sound: as of the nightingale too far off to be heard" and "*e l'olors—* / The smell of that place— *d'enoi ganres*" (*XX* 90). See also Hugh Kenner, *The Pound Era* (Berkeley: University of California Press, 1973), 116. By keeping Arnaut's language here, Pound's own poem becomes a sound "too far off to be heard," and the smell that banishes sadness must be surmised from the final lines of this passage, again encrusted with a Provençal word: "And the light falls, *remir*, / From her breast to thighs." Pound's ways with translation are varied, and in this short passage we can see how he offers the original and a translation in the first example, and in the second includes a word that can be elided in our reading of the complete sense. Again, see *The Pound Era*, 118–20.

10. Michael Bernstein, *The Tale of the Tribe: Ezra Pound and the Modern Verse Epic* (Princeton: Princeton University Press, 1980), 38–39.

11. Michael Harper, "Truth and Calliope: Ezra Pound's Malatesta," *PMLA* 96 (January 1981): 99.
12. Kenner, *The Pound Era*, 428.
13. Joseph N. Riddel, "Pound and the Decentered Image," *The Georgia Review* 29 (Fall 1975): 590.
14. Kenner, *The Pound Era*, 416–19.
15. Bernstein, *The Tale of the Tribe*, 29–74.
16. Wendy Stallard Flory, *Ezra Pound and The Cantos: A Record of Struggle* (New Haven: Yale University Press, 1980), 182.
17. For a discussion of Pound's interest in natural language, see David Simpson, "Pound's Wordsworth; or Growth of a Poet's Mind," *ELH* 45 (Winter 1978): 660–86.

6. *Conclusion*

1. The question will certainly arise: why is Wallace Stevens not discussed here as a major poet who wrote long poems? The answer is that he was in an earlier version, but the problems he poses and the structure of his career as a constant struggle with a variety of long poems made his case so different that I had to concede with a great reluctance that he required special treatment, which perhaps I will give him at another time.
2. See Renato Poggioli, *The Theory of the Avant-Garde* (Cambridge: Harvard University Press, 1968), for a discussion of the antagonistic movements in Modernism.
3. de Man, *Blindess and Insight*, 147.
4. Charles Baudelaire from "Theophile Gautier," excerpted in Richard Ellmann et al., eds., *The Modern Tradition: Backgrounds of Modern Literature* (New York: Oxford University Press, 1965), 101–2.
5. Lionel Trilling, "On the Modern Element in Modern Literature," in Irving Howe, ed., *Literary Modernism* (Greenwich, Conn.: Fawcett Publications, Inc., 1967), 78.
6. de Man, 168.
7. See, for example, Delmore Schwartz, "T. S. Eliot as the International Hero," in *Literary Modernism*, 277–85.

Index

Aeneid, 85
Altieri, Charles, 164–65n
St. Augustine, 42

The Barb of Time, 168n
Baudelaire, Charles, 35, 36, 156, 169n
Benzi, Andreas, 125
Bernstein, Michael, 123, 124, 130, 168n, 169n
The Bible, 136
Blindness and Insight: Essays in the Rhetoric of Contemporary Criticism, 164n, 169n
Bollard, Margaret L., 167n
Browning, Robert, 111, 112, 113, 115, 167n
Buddha, 42

Burke, Kenneth, 84–85
Bush, Ronald, 110, 167–68n

Canello, 118
Commentaries (Pope Pius II), 119, 125
A Companion to the Cantos of Ezra Pound, 168n
The Confessions of St. Augustine, 42
Confucius, 136
Crane, Hart, 1, 2, 3, 7, 9, 10, 11, 12, 14, 16, 17, 19, 20, 45, 47–76, 77, 78, 87, 101, 109, 111, 112, 117, 149, 152, 154, 155, 156, 158, 159, 160, 165n, 166n
  "Atlantis," 47, 48, 50, 51, 53, 56, 61, 62, 63, 64, 65, 69,

74, 75, 76, 101, 166n
"Ave Maria," 57, 59, 60, 61,
  64, 69
The Bridge, 7, 10, 14, 19, 20,
  21, 46, 47–76, 89–90, 101,
  109, 149, 154, 155, 165n
"The Broken Tower," 55
"To Brooklyn Bridge," 48
"Cape Hatteras," 67, 72, 73,
  111
"Cutty Sark," 57, 67, 68, 69
"The Dance," 57, 59, 63, 64,
  65, 69, 70
"Harbor Dawn," 57, 63, 69–70
"Indiana," 63, 67, 72
"National Winter Garden," 67
"Powhatan's Daughter," 63, 64
"Proem," 61, 64, 76
"Quaker Hill," 72, 73, 74
"The River," 57, 63, 69, 70, 72
"Southern Cross," 66
"Three Songs," 57, 59, 66
"The Tunnel," 57, 59, 61, 63,
  64
"Van Winkle," 63, 72
"Virginia," 66
White Buildings, 165n
Crosby, Caresse and Harry, 72
Curie, Marie, 100

Daniel, Arnaut, 29, 118, 158
Dante Alighieri, 7, 107
Davie, Donald, 168n
Day, John, 36
Death in Venice, 161
The Death of Ivan Ilytch, 161

De Man, Paul, 152, 163–64n,
  169n
Derrida, Jacques, 167n
Dickinson, Emily, 3
Divus, 136
Doeren, Suzanne Clark, 165n
Douglas, Clifford Hugh, 6, 145
Dryden, John, 22, 24, 33, 164n
Duncan, Isadora, 74

Elegantiae linguae latinae, 115
Eliot, T. S., 1, 2, 3, 6, 8, 10, 12,
  13, 17, 18–46, 48, 55, 81,
  108, 109, 112, 115, 119, 121,
  122, 135, 136, 143, 150, 151,
  154, 155, 156, 157, 158, 159,
  160, 164n, 165n, 168n
"Ash Wednesday," 164n
"The Burial of the Dead," 35,
  38, 40
"Death by Water," 27, 32, 42,
  43
"The Death of St. Narcissus,"
  39
"The Fire Sermon," 22, 23, 24,
  25, 32, 36, 40, 41, 42, 43
Four Quartets, 24, 78
"He Do the Police in Different
  Voices (1): Part 1," 32
"He Do the Police in Different
  Voices: Part II," 32
The Waste Land, 2, 5, 6, 7, 10,
  18–46, 48, 55, 109, 115, 119,
  121, 136, 149, 150, 153, 155,
  157, 158, 164n, 165n
"What the Thunder Said,"
  23–24, 25, 32, 33, 38, 43

Eliot in His Time, 164n, 165n
Ellmann, Richard, 169n
Ezra Pound: Poet as Sculptor, 168n
Ezra Pound and the Cantos: A Record of Struggle, 169n

Fenollosa, Ernest Francisco, 142
Fiero, F. Douglass, 166n
Fire Sermon (Buddha), 42
Fitzgerald, Edward, 7
Flory, Wendy Stallard, 133, 169n
Ford, Ford Madox, 142
The Form of the Unfinished: English Poetics from Spenser to Pound, 164n
Frank, Joseph, 12, 13, 16, 164n
Frank, Waldo, 51, 57, 58
Frazer, Sir James, 38, 39
From Ritual to Romance, 6, 33, 165n

Gall, Sally M., 163n, 166n
Gardner, Helen, 164n
The Genesis of Ezra Pound's Cantos, 110, 167n
Geographic, 88
Götterdämmerung, 42
Gregory, Horace, 83

Hall, Donald, 164n
Harmon, William, 165n
Harper, Michael, 123, 124, 169n
Hart Crane, 166n
Heart of Darkness, 161
Heydon, John, 142
Holy Guide, 142
Homer, 7, 130
Howe, Irving, 169n

Irwin, John, 166n

James, Henry, 9
Joyce, James, 31, 115, 168n

Kahn, Otto, 51, 52, 68, 70, 165n
Kenner, Hugh, 21, 24, 25, 123–24, 129, 164n, 165n, 168n, 169n

Laforgue, Jules, 3
Langbaum, Robert, 165n
The Last Puritan, 94
Leaves of Grass, 8, 58
Levy, Emil, 118, 168n
Lewis, R. W. B., 50–51, 66, 166n
Literary Modernism, 169n
Litz, A. Walton, 164n

The Magic Mountain, 161
Malatesta, Sigismundo, 115–20, 122–29, 143, 169n
Mallarmé, Stéphane, 13
Manes, 135
Mapping Literary Modernism: Time and Development, 163n
Mariani, Paul, 167n
Marvell, Andrew, 22, 36
Medici, Alessandro, 120
Medici, Lorenzo, 120
Melville, Herman, 70
Miller, J. Hillis, 166n
The Modern Poetic Sequence: The Genius of Modern Poetry, 163n
The Modern Tradition: Backgrounds of Modern Literature, 169n
Munch, Gerhart, 138

Munson, Gorham, 19
Mussolini, Benito, 133, 134, 135

Nietzsche, Friedrich, 166n
Notes from the Underground, 161

The Odyssey, 11, 136
Omar Khayyam, 7
Oxford Book of Modern Verse, 155

Paige, D. D., 167n
Paradise Lost, 32
Parsifal, 36
Pascal, Blaise, 24
Pearlman, Daniel, 168n
Pease, Donald, 165n
Perloff, Marjorie, 119
The Pocket Book of Verse, 136
Poe, Edgar Allan, 3, 47, 58, 62, 75
The Poetics of Indeterminacy, 119
The Poetry of Hart Crane, 166n
Poets of Reality, 166n
Poggioli, Renato, 169n
Pope, Alexander, 22, 33, 82
Pope Pius II, 119, 125, 126, 128
Pound, Ezra, 1, 2, 6–7, 8, 9, 10, 11, 12, 13, 15, 16, 17, 19, 21, 22, 23, 32, 33, 35, 42, 43, 45, 49, 79, 80, 97, 106–47, 149, 150, 151, 152, 153, 154, 155, 159, 160, 161, 164n, 167n, 168n, 169n
  "Arnaut Daniel," 168n
  Canto I, 17, 114, 136
  Canto III, 129
  Canto IV, 115, 129
  Canto V, 115

  Canto VI, 115
  Canto VII, 119, 120, 122, 130, 143
  Canto VIII, 115, 118, 128
  Canto IX, 128
  Canto X, 128
  Canto XI, 128
  Canto XIII, 151
  Canto XIV, 129
  Canto XX, 118
  Canto XLVI, 131
  Canto LXXIV, 138, 140
  Canto LXXV, 138
  Canto LXXVI, 138
  Canto LXXIX, 140
  Canto LXXXI, 141
  Canto LXXXV, 141
  Canto XC, 142
  Canto XCIII, 142
  The Cantos, 5, 6, 13, 14, 19, 21, 46, 106–47, 149, 150, 153, 154, 155, 157, 160, 167n, 168n
  A Draft of XVI Cantos, 107, 129
  A Draft of XXX Cantos, 107
  The Drafts and Fragments, 142
  Drafts and Fragments of Cantos CX–CXVII, 3
  Guide to Kulchur, 107, 120
  "Hugh Selwyn Mauberley," 22
  "Notes for CXVII *et seq.*," 17
  Pisan Cantos, 133, 134, 137, 140, 145
  Poetry Canto I, 111, 113, 140, 146
  Poetry Canto II, 114
  Poetry Canto III, 114
  Poetry Cantos, 112, 114, 136, 167n

"The Renaissance," 115
Rock-Drill, 141
Selected Cantos, 113
Thrones, 141, 143
The Pound Era, 168n, 169n
The Prelude, 32
Purgatorio, 42

Quinones, Ricardo J., 163n

Rajan, Balachandra, 164n
Ramsey, Roger, 166n
Reactionary Essays on Poetry and Ideas, 165n
Remembering Poets: Reminiscences and Opinions, 164n
Riddel, Joseph, 124, 125, 165n, 167n, 169n
Rosenthal, M. L., 163n, 166n
Rowe, John Carlos, 166n
Rudge, Olga, 138

Santayana, George, 94
Sappho, 34
Schelling, Felix, 7
Schwartz, Delmore, 169n
Simpson, David, 169n
Sordello, 111
Spenser, Edmund, 164n
Stevens, Wallace, 66, 77, 169n
Stieglitz, Alfred, 55
Studies of the Greek Poets, 89, 157
Sundquist, Eric J., 166n
Symonds, John Addington, 89, 157

The Tale of the Tribe: Ezra Pound and the Modern Verse Epic, 168n, 169n

Tate, Allen, 49, 165n
The Tempest, 36, 42
Tennyson, Alfred, 30
Terrell, Carroll, 118, 168n
"Theophile Gautier," 169n
The Theory of the Avant-Garde, 169n
Trials of the Word, 166n
Trilling, Lionel, 161, 162, 169n
Tristan and Isolde, 39

Ulysses, 115
Unterecker, John, 165n
Upanishad, 25
Uroff, Margaret Dickie, 165n

Valla, Lorenzo, 114, 115
Villon, François, 7
Virgil, 15, 82, 85

Wagner, Richard, 30
Weber, Brom, 166n
Weston, Jessie L., 30, 31, 38, 165n
Whitman, Walt, 3, 8, 58, 75, 92, 133, 152, 160
The Widening Gyre: Crisis and Mastery in Modern Literature, 164n
William Carlos Williams: A New World Naked, 167n
Williams, William Carlos, 1, 2, 3, 7, 9, 11, 12, 13, 14, 15, 17, 20, 45, 77–105, 109, 112, 113, 117, 148, 149, 151–52, 153, 154, 155, 156, 157, 159, 160, 166n, 167n, 168n
"The Delineaments of the Giants," 81

The Great American Novel, 78
"An Idyl," 100
In the American Grain, 84, 168n
"The Library," 93, 96
Paterson, 1, 5, 7, 11, 14, 15, 20, 21, 46, 77–105, 110, 113, 149, 153, 154, 155, 157, 166n, 167n
"Paterson," 166n
Paterson I, 78, 79, 83, 86, 89, 90, 91, 95
Paterson II, 84, 91, 95, 97
Paterson III, 14, 93, 95, 97, 98, 102
Paterson IV, 100, 103
Paterson V, 79, 104, 154, 167n
"Paterson: Episode 17," 93
"Prologue to *Kora in Hell*," 77
"The Run to the Sea," 100
Spring & All, 3, 14, 149, 154
"Sunday in the Park," 91, 92, 93, 96
Winters, Yvor, 165n
Wordsworth, William, 169n

Yeats, William Butler, 155